GREEN'S
NOT BLACK &
WHITE

GREEN'S NOT BLACK & WHITE

Dominic Muren

First edition for the United States, its territories
and dependencies, and Canada published in 2009
by Barron's Educational Series, Inc.

© 2009 by Ivy Press Limited

This book was conceived, designed, and produced by
Ivy Press
210 High Street,
West Street,
Lewes, East Sussex, BN7 2NS, U.K.

All inquiries should be addressed to:
Barron's Educational Series, Inc.
250 Wireless Boulevard
Hauppauge, NY 11788
www.barronseduc.com

ISBN-13: 978-0-7641-4248-2
ISBN-10: 0-7641-4248-8

Library of Congress Control Number: 2008937794

Creative Director: Peter Bridgewater
Publisher: Jason Hook
Editorial Director: Tom Kitch
Art Director: Wayne Blades
Senior Project Editor: Polita Caaveiro
Project Designer: Kate Haynes
Designer: Jon Raimes
Artwork: Melvyn Evans
Reviewer: Reuben Deumling

Printed in China
9 8 7 6 5 4 3 2 1

This book is printed on recycled paper

CONTENTS

INTRODUCTION

The green movement began life as a tiny seed, sown by Rachel Carson in 1962 with the publication of her book *Silent Spring*. Planted in a bed laid down by writers and naturalists such as George Perkins Marsh, Henry David Thoreau, and John Muir, this seed—a terrifying reality check about the damage that industrial chemicals and pesticides such as DDT were doing to food chains and whole ecosystems—took root, and began to grow. Progress was slow at first, as it can be with new growth, but year by year, leaf by leaf, the fledgling green movement spread. In 1972, Carson's chemical antagonist DDT was banned in the United States. Just over a decade later, CFCs, implicated in a newly formed ozone hole, were also strictly controlled. Recycling programs became commonplace. The 1980s saw education campaigns about endangered species, rainforest ecology, and water conservation being taught in primary school. The 1990s saw those kids and their parents begin to vote for real change in these areas, both with their ballots and with their dollars.

Even in light of all this growth, the last few years have been spectacular—a blossoming of the movement that Carson would never have believed would happen only thirty years later. The Kyoto Protocol was ratified by all but the most backward-looking nations, and a subsequent agreement promises to be even better. A climate change awareness advocate won the Nobel Peace Prize. Perhaps most important, consumers have begun to demand eco-friendly choices in their shopping, and the market has responded strongly.

So, you may be surprised when I tell you, with the green movement in its peak, that humans need to stop worrying about destroying the earth. Please keep reading; this is not a joke. The idea that humanity will destroy nature through pollution and overharvesting is simply wrong. It is certainly an understandable position to take; after all, the seed from which all this growth came was a cautionary tale about the damage that human endeavor can do to nature. But even hundreds of thousands of times the DDT, or nuclear waste, or greenhouse gas, or any other pollutant that has already been released, would not destroy nature. Bacteria eat everything from rotten meat to TNT, and even solid rock. Plants can grow on a volcanic island only months old. An asteroid 10 kilometers (6 miles) wide hit water off the coast of Mexico 65 million years ago, wiping out thousands of species, including the dinosaurs. Today, this area has some of the highest biodiversity in the world. Nature prevails.

No, humans need to stop worrying about destroying nature and start worrying about something more important: eliminating our place in nature. This is a subtle distinction, but a crucial one. The environmental movement has popularized a story where nature somehow exists because of our benevolence, rather than the other way around. A hundred years of fueling our lives, cars, farms, and technologies with fossil fuels have led us to believe that we are somehow capable of supporting ourselves without nature. In fact, the invisible pillars and strings of nature prop humans up like any other species. Even when we isolate ourselves from these direct linkages with nature—burning natural gas for heat instead of relying on the sun, fueling our plant growth with synthetic fertilizers instead of allowing them to produce at the levels that the soil normally supports—we are still deeply connected to natural systems. These attempts at disconnection often highlight our interconnection in dramatic, and dangerous, ways.

During these one hundred years of disconnection, there has been ample evidence of repercussions. In areas downwind from coal-burning power plants, acid rain kills trees and fish, and particulate matter increases incidence of asthma and lung diseases. Farmland treated heavily with pesticides and synthetic fertilizers experiences soil loss and reduced production. The waste products of industry are popping up in ever more personal places: lead from gasoline in our gardens, pesticide residue in our water, and dioxin, PCBs, and mercury in our own mothers' milk and blood. We have also seen declines in many of the natural pillars that support us: Deforestation has severely reduced our wood supply, and overfishing and pollution are damaging worldwide stocks of fish. Even our atmosphere seems to be refusing to continue maintaining the comfortable temperatures we have come to love, thrown out of balance by the massive amounts of CO_2 released by our efforts to establish ourselves as outside, even above, nature.

Indulging our delusions of control of nature, and attempting to enforce a disconnection from it, not only is obviously dangerous but probably seems like folly or bluster, something rational people just don't do. But, this is exactly what happens when we ask ourselves, "Will this local organic food I'm buying help save the earth?" Or, even more precariously, when we forgo the question altogether and assume that buying a pineapple labeled organic is preserving the planet for our children. We cannot save the earth; it does not need saving.

The future safety, health, and comfort of humanity depend not on saving nature but on recognizing, reinforcing, and strengthening our relationship with it. While this change in stance is not a large one, it requires something fundamentally different: thought. Saving something is as easy as checking to see if your action hurts it; reinforcing a relationship requires understanding the existing relationship, and the effect of the choice at hand on that relationship. Making this judgment requires education and thoughtful consideration. This book aims to give you some of the former, and promote a good deal more of the latter. While occasionally you will be provided with the suggestion "your best option is," more often you will be on your own to choose, based on the presented information, which course of action will help reinforce the kind of natural system that best supports your life.

While many answers will be similar for many people, many will be vastly different. Consider how absurd an idea it is that buying Alaskan salmon in Seattle and buying Alaskan salmon in Sydney could have the same environmental consequences. Location matters. Your economic situation matters. Many things factor in to your decision and influence which choices are available to you, and which are most effective for you. You are the best person to decide how a choice will affect you; no one knows you better. Above all, your decision should be a decision—a resolution of the things you consider important—and not the result of some environmental dogma or marketing. You will need to learn more about the facts of your choices than this book can tell (some suggestions for this are included in the conclusion and appendices). You will need to think more about your choices than most people (especially marketers) would like you to. You may have to adopt new values, abandon old traditions, or form entirely new ones. It will not be simple. But it will be worth it. What purpose can be more important than to ensure your own safety and the safety of those important to you? These are the stakes of the choices in this book, and in the choices in your life, every day.

CHAPTER ONE

FOOD

What more fundamental connection could there be between humans and nature than the things that we grow for food? The food we eat comes from the plants, animals, and ecosystems that make up the complex and dynamic system we call nature. Therefore, something as simple as buying a bottle of wine has consequences as varied as fungicides being sprayed on vineyards in Australia, cork forests being saved from becoming farmland in southern Spain, and diesel fuel being burned to get the wine to a store in England. The choices that we make in the grocery store and when dining out have the potential to influence not only our health, but also the way that our food is grown, raised, or caught, and by extension, how consistent or self-sustaining that food system is. Making choices to ensure safe, consistent, nourishing food is a crucial part of saving our place in nature.

BUY ORGANIC?

YES...

The most visible part of the green movement is perhaps the push toward growing and eating organic food. What "organic" means varies depending on what country the food is sold in. In general, it is regulated to be grown without synthetic fertilizers or pesticides, many of which have been proven dangerous for humans and ecosystems.

■ Farmers benefit, because prolonged exposure to synthetic pesticides can lead to health problems. The World Health Organization (WHO) estimates that one to five million cases of pesticide poisoning occur worldwide among agricultural workers each year, with approximately 20,000 fatalities.[1,2]

■ Ecosystems benefit, because synthetic fertilizer runoff encourages algae to grow, causing dangerously low oxygen levels everywhere from small local lakes to the Gulf of Mexico and the Black Sea.[3]

■ Customers benefit, because not only are they exposed to fewer pesticide residues, but the organic foods that they eat have higher concentrations of vitamins and antioxidants than their conventionally grown counterparts.[4]

BUT...

Because of its restrictions, organic farming can be more expensive than conventional, which may encourage farmers to locate their operations in faraway countries where labor is cheaper, or where an ideal climate is available all year round.

■ Shipping organic food from faraway growing locations may significantly increase its energy footprint, resulting in higher greenhouse gas emissions per calorie of food.

■ Nonlocal organic production also bleeds money from your community into faraway economies, rather than supporting local farmers who can make your local community more sustainable in the event of a crisis.

■ In addition, while synthetic pesticides are banned in organic food, natural pesticides are often allowed, and some, such as copper and sulfur salts, are still very toxic, despite being "organic."

■ Finally, some foods such as fish[5,6] and milk[7] have definitions of organic that may not mean they are chemical free. There are loopholes in the definition that allow for things such as non-organic-certified feed, or unhealthy living conditions.

BUY LOCAL?

YES...

Even if it's not organic produce, buying local produce has significant benefits for environmental health, as well as personal and community health.

■ Buying from local farmers can reduce the amount of energy used in transporting food to your table, especially if you live near the farm from which you are purchasing.

■ Supporting local farming encourages local self-sufficiency, which can make the difference in case of natural disaster or fluctuation in the price of fuel (and therefore the price of long-distance food).

■ Local farmers can more easily accept feedback from their customers about what kind of food they want and how they want it grown. If people want organic, and make their demands clear enough, the farmer needs to start listening.

■ Finally, buying local can encourage a more seasonal, and therefore a fresher, diet of ripe food, compared with freighted foods, which are often picked unripe to avoid spoilage. These freighted foods are less nutritious.

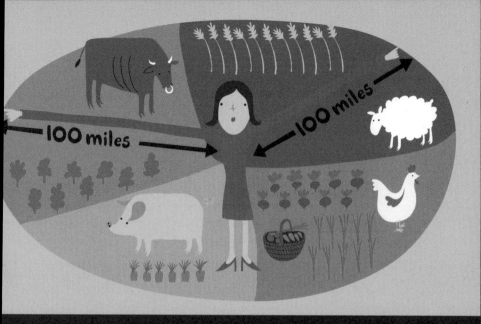

BUT...

"Food miles" shouldn't be the only factor determining where your food comes from. Many factors influence the environmental and social impacts of food, and decisions should be made on a per-case basis.

■ A recent study by DEFRA, the United Kingdom's environmental advisory body, found that tomatoes grown in greenhouses in the United Kingdom during the winter required three times more energy than those imported from Spain by road.[1]

■ Larger, more tightly packed ships and trucks used by supermarkets are often more efficient modes of transport than smaller, older trucks used by farmers to drive to markets. This applies especially to markets located in cities, where the distance may be farther from the farm.[2]

WHAT TO DO

Shop locally more often, but also shop seasonally to cut down on energy in hothouses. Consider using a local vegetable delivery service or Community Supported Agriculture (CSA) scheme to cut down on transportation.

EAT LESS MEAT?

YES...

While meat is a delicious (and often obligatory) component of modern meals, its environmental impacts may leave a different taste in the mouth.

■ Meat takes more calories to produce than any other kind of food, and so, for every meat-fed person, there could be multiple vegetable-fed people living on the same number of initial calories.

■ Factory farming practices associated with meat also produce significant amounts of methane (a greenhouse gas), nitrates, and ammonia runoff (a water pollutant that causes oxygen-poor "dead zones" in water bodies). One study found that 35–40 percent of anthropogenic methane production resulted from farmed animals or their waste.[1]

■ Factory farming of beef and chicken leads to greater incidence of food poisoning from antibiotic-resistant bacteria such as *E. coli*.

BUT...

The ways in which we currently produce meat are damaging to the environment, but the major environmental damage inflicted by meat-centered diets results more from the way we grow meat (factory farms and close-quarters pens) than from the meat itself.

■ In fact, if proper grazing practices are employed, cattle can be an effective method of ecosystem regeneration (especially in rangeland and prairie habitats). This can lead to greater biodiversity and ecosystem health, while producing meat with little or no input of fossil fuel.[2,3]

■ In countries with dense populations, hunting can be helpful (where lawful) and may be necessary to maintain healthy, controlled populations of deer, rabbits, and geese in the absence of predators.

■ Finally, animals such as pigs[4] and goats[5] can be effectively used to dispose of food waste and control weeds while producing high-quality food.

> **WHAT TO DO**
>
> Consider meat a flavoring agent—bacon on salad—rather than the main event. Choose "beyond organic" meat, raised using methods that strengthen local ecosystems and watersheds.

YES...

Through modern processing, corn, soybeans, and the food they are processed into make up a major percentage of the calories eaten by those in developed countries. Even things you might not expect include ingredients made from corn—such as soda, fried chicken, ground meat, and even French fries.[1] But high usage of corn has serious environmental repercussions.

■ Cultivating corn strips nutrients from the soil that must be replaced, or the soil will eventually become unusable.

■ Corn's minimal root system and spaced planting needs do little to slow the flow of rain running off of fields, resulting in soil loss. This is made worse by heavy tillage—plowing of the soil—when corn is replanted. Worldwide, 100,000 square kilometers (about 38,610 square miles) of farmland is unworkable because of soil loss each year.[2]

■ Growing corn requires massive fossil fuel inputs, particularly in producing synthetic fertilizers to speed its growth, and in the steps required for drying, to make it suitable for shipping.[3]

BUT...

Corn can be produced efficiently; it is the way in which it is grown and the scale of production that make it environmentally dangerous.

■ Corn has been grown selectively for centuries to survive well in cultivation and produces very high yields per acre of cultivated crops, even if no synthetic fertilizers are used.

■ Corn can be made into a number of nutritious whole foods (nonprocessed foods) such as sweet corn, hominy, flour, and breads like tortillas.

■ Polyculture plantings of corn and other plants, such as in the Central American milpas, allow for large amounts of food, supplying a complete nutritional requirement to be produced in a very small acreage.

WHAT TO DO

Eat more whole foods, or those free from processing, such as fresh vegetables, wholegrain bread and pasta, cheese, and meats. As Michael Pollan states in *In Defense of Food*, "If you read an ingredient that your grandmother would not recognize, you probably shouldn't eat it."

Eat Less Corn?

EAT LESS FISH?

YES...

Despite the overwhelming area of the earth's surface that is covered by water, and the huge populations of plants and animals capable of living there, fisheries around the world are seriously depleted—or on the verge of collapse—because of overfishing.

■ High-value fish, such as salmon, sushi-grade tuna, and sea bass, are often caught far from markets, frozen, and flown long distances, which requires significant energy expenditures. Sushi served in New York may have been caught off the coast of Australia, flown to Tsukiji market in Japan for sale, purchased, and then flown to New York to be served.[1]

■ Low-value fish, such as shrimp, are caught in trawling operations with large amounts of bycatch, which can include important ecosystem members such as small fish, eels, and even sea turtles.[2]

■ Farmed fish introduces waste products, antibiotics, and parasites into wild stocks of fish, damaging their health, and reducing populations. Fish farms need large amounts of wild, herbivorous fish to feed to the carnivorous fish—salmon, tuna—that we eat.[3]

Food

BUT...

The worldwide fishing industry is an important activity that we can't afford to lose. It also has the potential to affect the environment positively.

■ Fish is an important source of protein for coastal communities all over the world. The desire to preserve this resource can serve as a powerful motivation for sustainable fishing practices.

■ Similarly, pressure to preserve fish stocks also puts pressure on preserving their habitats and related species, which serves to strengthen the environment as a whole.

■ Land-based farm raising of freshwater fish such as tilapia and catfish can produce more protein with less waste than chicken or cattle operations. Cattle require 7 kilograms (about 15 pounds) of grain to produce 1 kilogram (about 2 pounds) of meat, while tilapia can produce the same for just 2 kilograms (about 4 pounds) of grain feed.4

WHAT TO DO
Choose fish that are herbivores, like tilapia, over carnivores like swordfish. Avoid ocean-based fish farming. Check online for updated information about what fish are best.

GROW YOUR OWN FOOD?

YES...

What better way to ensure that you know what your food is doing to the environment than to grow it yourself? Growing food is an empowering experience, and it can increase your understanding of what is required for food cultivation.

■ Growing your own food cuts transportation energy expenditures to a minimum. It probably involves just you, a basket full of vegetables, and the walk from the garden.

■ You know exactly what chemicals and fertilizers you use on your own crops. You can use organic pest controls and compost, or skip pesticides altogether.

■ Watering and fertilizing a garden instead of a lawn puts those resources to better use. According to one study carried out in the United States, 30–60 percent of urban freshwater is used to water lawns.[1]

■ Perhaps most important, growing your own food gives you a much better idea of the issues involved in letting somebody else do it, and might lead to better oversight if you do choose to buy food from other producers.

BUT...

As with individual production of anything, individual food production carries with it significant inefficiencies. Just as you are more productive at your job because you are skilled at it, farmers who spend all their time farming can produce more food.

■ Specialized producers can grow more food on less land, leaving more space potentially undeveloped.

■ Trying to grow significant amounts of food sustainably in dense urban areas is difficult, and a move to grow more of our own food could increase the desire for suburban housing and the inefficiencies of transportation that system brings. Lawns and garden space were cited by residents as reasons for moving to Levittown, the first major post-World War II suburb of New York.[2]

■ Specialized organic farmers have access to complex natural pest-control methods and compost-based fertilizers, and are less likely to resort to synthetic fertilizers from the home and garden store (as home growers might be)

SAY NO TO GMOs?

YES...

Genetically modified organisms (GMOs)—plants or animals whose genetic material has been directly altered by scientists using modern genetic techniques—present a number of scenarios in which they could cause damage to consumers, and to the environment.

■ Genes that allow plants to produce their own pesticides, such as BT in corn (called BT-corn), can generate pollen or leaf litter, which can, in theory, have a negative impact on beneficial insects in nonagricultural ecosystems.[1]

■ Genetic manipulations alter the proteins present in food plants, which can result in novel food allergens and unexpected allergic reactions when consumed.[2]

■ Finally, GMO plants with weedy relatives—such as commercial rape seed and weedy wild mustard—may interbreed to create weedy offspring with more powerful traits, including pesticide resistance. These "superweeds" could become invasive and do damage in nonagricultural ecosystems.[1]

BUT...

The truth is that people have been modifying organisms for agriculture since agriculture began.

■ Hybrid crops (those genetically modified by intensive breeding, rather than by direct manipulation) can increase the yield per acre of crops by many times, which decreases the need for farmland, fertilizer, and pesticides. Often, directly modifying a plant's genes takes less time than breeding, so better plants can be made faster.

■ GMO crops with pest resistance or pesticidal properties greatly decrease the amount of chemicals needed to grow them. For example, China's cultivation of BT transgenic cotton had, by 2001, reduced pesticide use by 78,000 tons per year.[3]

■ Most important, it is thought that much more damage to biodiversity and species health is done by the vast, monocultural way in which we farm than by any gene we have yet released into the wild through breeding or modern biotechnology.

CHAPTER TWO

SHOPPING

We've made tools since before the beginning of civilization and we've probably traded with each other for the tools we wanted for just as long. So, it should be no surprise that shopping has a huge part to play in the damage we do to our relationship with the environment. In the past, reckless natural resource usage practices meant that wonderful things such as tortoiseshell eyeglasses, feathered caps, and even, in some cases, solid wood furniture became scarce, or unavailable. Now, our globalized markets mean that shopping at the local department store for a mundane wooden desk or wool scarf can result in deforestation of rainforest in Thailand, or threaten the survival of wild goat herds on the Tibetan plateau. Even something as simple as choosing a similar product that is 10 percent cheaper or more expensive can mean the difference between a product shipped over oceans or one made down the street. Shopping choices decide how much or how little nature will support your efforts to have all that you need.

CONSIDER "EMBODIED ENERGY"?

YES...

One method gaining popularity for determining the sustainability credentials of products is to try to quantify the energy it took to make and transport them to you —that is, their "embodied energy."

■ Shipping to point of sale can add a significant amount of energy to the total of a product. Also, think about the constituent parts of the product. For example, a cell phone might have plastic from the United States, tantalum from Africa,[1] and chips from Singapore, all assembled in China before being shipped to you in New York.

■ The materials something is made from can significantly influence the energy needed to make it. The difference in energy between a 4-kilogram (9-pound) chair in wood (10 megajoules) and aluminum (908 megajoules) would run a laptop for 400 days.[2]

■ The forming process used to make a product also has a huge bearing on its embodied energy. Materials that require high temperatures, such as ceramics and glass, require more energy than low-temperature materials such as cloth, paper, and wood.

BUT...

It's not just how much energy it took to make something, but how much use you will get out of that energy (the product's embodied energy per use).

■ Some materials are more durable than others. A plywood chair might only last for 10 years, while a metal one could survive to be passed on to your grandchildren. Or a ceramic mug, while higher energy than a glass one, might last longer, since glass is more likely to break.

■ Some objects, such as paper picnicware, are designed to be disposable but may allow continued use. If you take lots of picnics, the total energy used to make all your plates could exceed the energy needed to make a reusable plastic or metal one.

■ The ability to repair an item can save significant energy when compared to buying a new one. Making products—especially electronics—that are repairable is an increasingly important part of minimizing the energy per use of a product.[3]

BUY CERTIFIED PRODUCTS?

YES...

Certification has become a popular way for companies to quickly reassure consumers of their green practices. Certification concerns have begun underwriting everything from lumber, to food, to clothing.

■ Organic labels give companies a chance to show off their otherwise invisible good deeds, and put pressure on competitors to win your business.

■ Organic labels help customers to assign a value to sustainable practices. For example, sales of USDA-certified organic produce in the United States grew by 24 percent between 2005 and 2006 despite costing significantly more per pound.[1] This sends a strong message to the market.

■ Labeling also saves you time when deciding which products align with your values. The less frustration you face when shopping, the less likely you will be to compromise in the interest of just being finished.

BUT...

Remember that a certification seal is only as good as the entity certifying it, and the standards that are required to achieve that seal. As a purchaser, you need to be aware of which certification schemes may be sketchy, and what each scheme means in terms of real results.

WHAT TO DO

Be skeptical of any label that claims eco-credentials until you can check it out online.

■ Some labels, such as "natural," "grass-fed," or "free-range," may be minimally or completely unregulated in your country. For example, in the United States, cage-free eggs must simply come from hens not living in cages, but the standard says nothing about living density, access to the outdoors, or sanitation conditions.[2]

■ Other certifications, like those for wood, are difficult to police. Many logging operations for this certified wood are carried out in extremely remote areas. After the wood is milled, it is impossible to trace back to a certain logging site. Mistaken certification and outright bribery have both been known to occur.[3]

YES...

The answer, in a consumption-driven economy, is often to buy more of the "good stuff." If advertising is to be believed, the good stuff is fair-trade organic silk blouses and grass-fed beef. Buying more of it will save not only you, but the environment itself.

■ If more consumers buy organic food, or lead-free electronics, then industry produces fewer environmental toxins. This is a crucial point, since a large percentage of toxic waste and greenhouse gas emissions are generated by industry.

■ If consumer demand for eco-friendly products goes up, then more companies will switch to these kinds of manufacturing methods, which should drive prices down.

■ Finally, the waste we make when we throw these products out will be less toxic for the environment and for us.

BUT...

Excessive consumption of products, and the waste that this generates—whether products are green or not—is a big part of our environmental problems. Buying fewer things in general is also crucial to minimizing these problems.

■ Fewer products equates to a smaller carbon footprint because of reduced shipping and manufacturing energy.

■ Fewer products also translates into less waste from packaging, and from discarded items. In the European Union, packaging waste accounts for about 15 percent of municipal waste by weight, and 20–30 percent by volume.[1]

■ If you buy fewer things, you can afford to buy higher-quality things, which will last longer, giving more uses per energy used to manufacture them.

WHAT TO DO
Buying fewer products is important, especially in the West, where overconsumption of resources is most pronounced.

DO SOME ECO-REMODELING ?

YES...

Our homes are where we spend the bulk of our energy, our money, and, hopefully, a large portion of our time. Making your home more eco-sensitive can add up to big environmental benefits.

■ Using efficient electrical appliances such as modern water heaters and washing machines can save huge amounts of energy. Recent innovations such as tankless water heaters and drain heat recovery systems can both reduce water-heating energy by 30 percent.[1]

■ Low-flow showerheads, and low-flush toilets can significantly reduce water consumption in your home. A study conducted in Seattle, Washington, found that a family of four that replaced their kitchen and bathroom faucets with low-flow attachments could save 1,700 gallons (6,433 liters) of water per year.[2]

■ Modern multi-paned windows can significantly reduce heat loss during the winter, and help to hold in the cool if you have an your air conditioner in the summer, resulting in lower energy requirements.

Shopping

BUT...

Before you install new bamboo flooring or Syndecrete countertops, consider whether you can get the same visual impact without as many new materials.

■ Renovations, even if carried out using eco-friendly materials, generate significant waste, and may not confer any real lasting ecological benefits. The European Union generates 1.8 billion tons of waste per year, and 25 percent is generated by construction, demolition, and remodeling projects.[3]

■ New materials such as flooring and furniture require resources to be made and energy to be shipped to you.

■ Newly applied paints and glues can release volatile organic compounds (VOCs) and other unpleasant chemicals into your home for years after a renovation.

WHAT TO DO

Consider rearranging furniture, refinishing your floor, painting walls, using reclaimed lumber or building materials, or swapping items on Freecycle or Craigslist. The less new stuff you get, the less energy you use, and the less old stuff ends up in a landfill.

USE PAPER BAGS?

YES...

WHAT TO DO

Reusable bags, no matter what they are made of, are better than paper or plastic, almost any way you consider it.

Possibly the oldest of environmental dilemmas, "paper or plastic" might just as well be "natural or synthetic." Certainly, if looked at this way, paper is a great choice.

■ Paper is completely biodegradable. Given two to five months of bacterial activity, a paper bag will be reduced to dirt.[1] And the best part of it is that no special composting is needed. Even if paper is left on the surface of the ground, bacteria will get to work on it eventually.

■ Paper is made from a renewable resource. Trees regrow, unlike the petroleum or natural gas needed for making plastic bags.

■ Another less apparent benefit of paper bags is that they cause less damage in the environment because of their fragility. For example, they are too fragile to cause starvation by blocking a sea turtle's stomach. And if they blow into a tree, they will not prevent its leaves from growing for years.[2]

BUT...

Because of differences in the way that plastic and paper bags are manufactured, when it comes to energy requirements and waste products, plastic bags also have significant advantages.

■ According to the American Plastics Council, it requires 30 percent less energy to manufacture two plastic bags than to manufacture one paper bag,[3] which means fewer greenhouse gas emissions.

■ Paper bags are more bulky and heavier than plastic bags; it takes seven trucks to deliver the same amount of paper bags as it takes one truck of plastic.[4] This would create additional greenhouse gas emissions.

■ Plastic bags require much less freshwater to produce than paper bags.[5]

■ Your best bet is to use a durable reusable bag that you can count on for hundreds of market trips.

MAKE PURCHASES ONLINE?

YES...

Recently, buying on the Internet has become a serious option for shoppers, and a serious opportunity for making eco-friendly buying choices.

■ Buying online can cut down on the amount of fuel used to transport your purchases from the manufacturer to you, because you can buy directly from the manufacturer. You can also choose a manufacturer whose production is located nearby. Often, products in large stores don't give this kind of information about place of origin, or how products are shipped and warehoused.

■ Buying online can also reduce packaging, since products don't have to look good on store shelves.

■ With the Internet's infinite selection, your purchases are more likely to match up with your particular level of eco-commitment, which helps reinforce the market in that direction, and can help shift more production in that direction.

BUT...

The Internet is a large, impersonal place, and it has the potential to be more secretive about the locations and processes involved in making products, especially given that Web information can fool buyers much more easily than holding a product in their hands.

■ Online shopping can open up retail locations that are far away without making you aware that the product will come from there.

■ National and worldwide person-to-person sales sites can increase total shipping, especially if you buy lots of small things individually. A major retail outlet would package all those items into one shipment, saving energy. Online purchases also encourage next-day shipping (by plane), which increases a product's embodied energy by 22 percent compared to ground shipping, the method that all big-box stores use to stock their shelves.[1]

■ Buying lots of small things individually online can easily dwarf the amount of shipping and packaging used to get the same number of items to a retail store.

CHAPTER THREE

ENERGY

Humans have long abandoned the old notion, "If you want something done right, you have to do it yourself." Long ago, we domesticated animals so we didn't have to do things ourselves—we still use expressions like "horsepower" that allude to this choice. But, just as we gave up our own hands for the hands and feet of animals, we have given up animal power for the energy locked away in fossil fuels. Where once a person worked for a week, and a horse for a day, we finish work in an hour by applying energy at staggering rates. Old notions have a way of clinging to their truth, though, even as technology marches forward. We've accomplished huge amounts of things, but mounting evidence of fossil fuel-induced pollution and climate change calls into question whether those things were done right, or whether our choices may have left us only borrowers who traded our horses for a mortgage that we couldn't pay back. Our energy choices today will decide whether we can again call on nature for help with our work, or whether we are doomed to find out what happens when our loan comes due.

USE CLEAN COAL?

YES...

"Clean coal" is a confusing term because its meaning has changed over the years. Until recently, it referred only to toxic emissions, not greenhouse gas ones.

■ Clean coal technologies include methods to clean minerals and impurities from the fuel before it is burned, limiting their release into the atmosphere.[1,2]

■ Clean coal technologies involve using steam to capture sulfur dioxide, which reduces this major cause of acid rain.[3]

■ Modern definitions of clean coal technology include provisions for capturing carbon from the waste gases, which, while commercially unproven, would potentially result in an energy source with zero greenhouse gas emissions.

> **WHAT TO DO**
> Avoid all types of fossil fuels where possible. If you have to use fossil fuel heat, choose either fuel oil or natural gas, which have fewer greenhouse emissions than coal.

BUT...

Clean coal is still coal, a fossil fuel that represents a huge amount of unreleased greenhouse gas emissions.

■ Coal produces less energy per CO_2 emission than any other fossil fuel, so even clean coal contributes more to the greenhouse effect than other fuels.

■ In order to keep costs down as labor costs go up, environmentally destructive mining methods such as "mountaintop removal" are being used to extract coal reserves. Even traditional underground mines can become unstable, leach toxins, and catch fire, years after being closed.[3]

■ Even the best clean coal technology does little to reduce mercury emissions from coal-based power generation, which account for 50 percent of the total emissions of the toxic metal in the United States.[4]

YES...

Electricity produced from wind is some of the most environmentally benign power currently available.

■ Modern turbines generate large amounts of power with one or two towers, instead of many smaller (and more expensive) towers, and so require less land. Often, the land can do double service as cropland or managed timberland, unlike other types of power plants, which require dedicated space.

■ Modern turbines turn at relatively low speeds, and therefore generate minimal noise, so they can be located near or even in cities. Recently a series of turbines was constructed near Atlantic City's urban center.

■ Most important, after the initial energy required to build the turbine, wind power is completely greenhouse gas-free.

WHAT TO DO

Wind power is one of the best options available for clean, sustainable power, so use it when you can, but do keep up to date with the latest options in eco-energy.

BUT...

If you're wondering why we aren't getting all our power from wind, there are good reasons, and they're not all about the cost.

■ Because the wind doesn't blow all day, every day, the power generated is intermittent.

■ Wind power doesn't map very well to energy needs. In most cases, winds are highest in the fall and winter when power is required for space heating, but electrical needs are also high in the summer, when power for air conditioning is required. Few cost-effective methods of energy storage on this scale exist.

■ Most important, few cities are located near high-wind areas, so energy losses during transmission of power can be high. While this is also true for coal and nuclear power transmission, this does add significantly to the cost of wind energy.

YES...

One piece of prevailing eco-wisdom is that if you can't trust the energy companies to give you clean, eco-friendly power, then you should make it yourself.

■ Installing a home system for generating power, such as a rooftop wind turbine or photovoltaics, can help you to generate a real portion of your own electrical energy.

■ Installing a combined heat and power (sometimes called cogeneration) system to provide heat and electricity for your home can achieve 90 percent efficiency (compared to 30–40 percent with a central power station) and a 30 percent reduction in fossil fuel emissions.[1]

■ Installing home power makes consumers more aware that energy is scarce, and doesn't just appear because you pay the electric bill. This may lead to a more informed public when it comes to society-level decisions.

BUT...

Putting up a windmill on your roof may not be the most economically effective way to reduce your energy usage.

■ In a typical UK home, 50 percent of heat loss occurs through poorly insulated walls and lofts.[2] Depending on the size of your home, adding this insulation probably costs less than any alternative energy source, and might end up being the equivalent of generating more power in energy savings.

■ According to the US Department of Energy, installing a tankless water heater can reduce your water-heating energy use by 24–34 percent. Since water heating represents 11 percent of total household energy use, this can be a significant energy gain, and still at a lower cost than most on-site power generation systems.[3]

YES...

Photovoltaics are one of the most unobtrusive ways to generate your own electricity.

■ They can easily be installed on an existing roof or garage, and they are virtually maintenance free once installed.

■ They can make you money if your municipality allows you to sell electricity back to the grid.

■ According to a study carried out by an Italian team of researchers, solar panels were completely carbon neutral—that is, they made back the energy embodied in their manufacture—in just two years.[1]

■ Perhaps the biggest plus is that they set a good example. Neighbors soon admire your fancy new solar cells and decide they want some of their own. Soon, keeping up with the Joneses becomes a positive thing, as more and more people choose clean energy.

BUT...

Like windmills, there are some very real reasons why we aren't roofing our houses in solar cells.

■ Solar cells are expensive. Traditional silicon cells are made with high-energy, high-precision processes identical to those used to make computer chips.

WHAT TO DO

Consider using solar hot water. It works in situations where less sunlight or diffuse sunlight is available. The costs are lower than for conventional water heating.

■ This high cost makes the power from solar cells around twice as expensive as coal-based electricity.[2] The same study that found that embodied energy paid back in two years also found that it took 20 years to pay back economically.[1]

■ While they are low maintenance, they do degrade over time. Modern cells can last up to twenty-five years, but they lose efficiency with age.

■ Finally, solar cells will only work in areas with sun, during times of the day when the sun is shining. Since many cities are intentionally located away from desert areas, they may not get enough hours of sunshine.

YES...

In its brief sixty-or-so years of life, nuclear energy has been hailed as the most dangerous creation of humanity. Despite the furor, nuclear has environmental benefits.

■ Ideally, because nuclear power releases energy stored inside internal bonds of atomic nuclei (rather than through a chemical reaction such as burning), the products of this reaction should be able to be contained completely. This means there is no pollution of any kind. Coal and natural gas cannot claim as much.

■ Since nuclear energy is not a fossil fuel, it does not produce CO_2, or any greenhouse gases, and therefore is an existing energy alternative that does not contribute to global warming.

■ Nuclear energy is a proven power-generation scheme with hundreds of operating installations around the world. Few other plausible non-fossil-fuel energy sources are so flexible, and none is so well tested.

BUT...

There is the ideal concept of a power source, and then there is the reality. Nuclear power has serious disadvantages from an environmental standpoint.

■ All nuclear reactions generate radioactive waste. This waste remains radioactive for thousands of years, and the cost of safely storing that type of material for that long has yet to be definitively determined. It may not be possible to "safely store" this material, since tens of thousands of years is beyond the scope of any government.

■ Similar technology for developing nuclear reactors allows the development of nuclear weapons. While nuclear war would be a significant human tragedy, it could potentially be a much greater environmental one.

■ Finally, excluding catastrophic toxicity, many toxins limit human capacity for leading healthy lives, and many radioactive compounds also limit human capacity for reproduction, leading to a collapse of the whole ecosystem. We just need to look at the repercussions of the catastrophe at Chernobyl in 1986.

CHOOSE TIDAL POWER?

YES...

Tidal power taps the energy stored in water flowing around the surface of the planet as it is dragged by the gravity of the moon. A number of different schemes for harnessing this power are under consideration, each with potential benefits.

■ First and foremost, a tidal energy system would have no exhaust emissions, which would create a carbon-neutral energy stream.

■ If a dam-type barrage of a tidal zone is used, the structure has the potential to mitigate flooding as well. A study carried out by the UK Sustainable Development Commission found that the Severn Barrage project on the Thames estuary would be useful backup flood protection, in addition to potentially generating 5 percent of the country's power.[1]

■ Large cities around the world are often located near tidal resources, as many of the world's biggest cities are built on bays or estuaries.

■ Tidal power is plentiful. An informal estimate of worldwide potential power published by Norway's Skatkraft energy group put it at 1,000 terawatt-hours[2]—enough to run one hundred million average US homes.

BUT...

As they say, the devil is in the details, and since the ocean touches so many lives, the details can get pretty complicated pretty fast.

■ Tidal power is expensive to install initially, but because of highly durable parts and limited wear, costs can be spread significantly over time. However, unlike solar power, the ocean can get very violent. As recent years have shown, global warming makes this violence less predictable. If the infrastructure needs to be replaced because of damage after only limited use, it can make tidal power very costly.

■ These installations need to alter the flow of tides in order to remove energy from them. In the case of dam-like structures, such as the proposed Severn Barrage, the structures can significantly impact fish populations. This is caused by blocking natural passages[3] for the fish, and may affect shellfish populations by changing high and low tide levels or tidal swings.[4]

CHOOSE HYDROELECTRIC POWER?

YES...

If burning fossil fuels is causing global warming, and nuclear energy may not be safe enough (despite being emission free), then what better solution than to use hydroelectric power to satisfy our energy needs?

■ Hydroelectric power is power generated by water as it flows down out of the mountains toward the oceans. As it goes over turbines it creates power without any combustion, and therefore produces no CO_2 emissions.

■ Damming rivers is a time-tested method for generating lots of electricity at a constant rate. This keeps costs down and stops customers from switching to coal or other fossil fuels.

■ Damming can also be used to alleviate seasonal variation in water supply, which can help communities avoid draining their groundwater and aquifers at unsustainable rates.

BUT...

Despite their innocuous appearance—they don't make smoke, or visible waste—dams have serious environmental impacts that you might not expect.

■ Like wind farms, dams are inconveniently located. Most cities are not situated in mountain passes where the best potential energy is located. Electricity has to be transported to where it is required, and some energy is lost in transmission.

■ Dams block the migration of fish such as salmon, which need to get from their ocean feeding grounds to their mountain breeding grounds near the end of their lives to reproduce.[1]

■ Dams can generate significant amounts of methane from trapped rotting vegetation in reservoirs, which acts as a greenhouse gas. One study found that the greenhouse emissions from the Curuá-Una dam in Pará, Brazil, were more than three-and-a-half times what would have been produced by generating the same amount of electricity from oil.[2]

CHAPTER FOUR

TRANSPORT &TRAVEL

If any form of technology has catalogued the transition of humans from our pre-industrial origins, through the industrial 20th century, to our present-day post-industrial, globalized world, it must be our technologies for transportation. Items that once were transported on the backs of donkeys, or in the holds of sailing ships, now make their trips in the holds of airplanes, or stacked ten stories tall on the decks of cargo freighters. The constant in all of these changing modes of transportation has been an increased trend to trade more energy for more speed. While speed seems an important—even essential—part of modern life, any trade that involves spending more energy usually means emitting more greenhouse gases. Climate change from greenhouse emissions is one of the greatest threats to humanity's prominent position in the natural supply chain. However, while transportation is a great place to cut ecological risks, its central place in modern society means that few of its dilemmas are easy decisions.

DRIVE A HYBRID?

YES...

A hybrid car combines space-age technology with hot new style to bring you a miracle! Other people think you are a good eco-citizen for driving it, and for good reason:

■ Hybrid cars are a twist on the classic internal combustion engine, which is very good at driving very fast for a very long time. In stop-and-go traffic, the efficiency of a standard engine goes down. To fix that, hybrids store electricity in a bank of batteries, and turn on an electric motor for low speeds or quick starts, increasing the efficiency of the engine.

■ Some hybrids have regenerative braking, which means that instead of slowing down by using friction to heat brake pads, they use the resistance from turning a generator to slow the wheels turning. This way, some of the energy it took to get the car moving can be reclaimed. This increases fuel efficiency and decreases emissions.

■ In the future, there is the prospect of plug-in hybrids, which would run mostly on batteries charged from household mains. An onboard engine would run the car in the event of long-distance driving.[1] Such a hybrid could be powered by solar, wind, or whatever electrical energy is available, making it potentially carbon neutral.

Transport & Travel

BUT...

Hybrids are by no means a panacea, as some have been led to believe. There are some real environmental drawbacks with the current state of the technology.

■ Hybrid vehicles have more engine components (an electric motor drive in addition to a gas engine), more electronic components (at least one additional computer), and a very large bank of high-quality batteries. This complexity makes for a car with both higher embodied energy and higher initial cost.

■ Depending on your driving habits, a different type of car may save you more energy. If you drive long distances at constant speeds, you will almost certainly save gas by buying a smaller, lighter car. Because a hybrid drivetrain is most efficient in stop-and-go traffic, the weight of the batteries will just hold you back on this kind of trip.

■ If you don't plan on driving much, you may be better off buying a smaller, lighter car, or getting membership in a car-share program. Because of the high embodied energy in the batteries of the car, if you don't drive it enough, you may not make back the energy you have already spent.

RIDE A BIKE?

YES...

If ecologically aware citizens had a logo, no doubt a bicycle would be part of it. Bikes are marvelous devices, and they have serious ecological benefits, as well as other benefits such as health and community-building.

■ Bikes take only a tiny amount of energy to make. Think about it in terms of a car. The lightest cars still weigh at least 6–8 times as much as the average person. Even a reasonably good bike only weighs a fraction of a person's weight. That means you are spending more energy transporting the human, and less transporting the bike.

■ Since bike riding is good exercise, riders experience health benefits such as a lower risk of heart disease. More important, since bike riders burn only food, they save trips to the gas station.

■ Bicycles allow cities to function more effectively by reducing the amount of urban space needed for transport. One single-occupant car requires 20 times the urban space of a cyclist.[1] That means that for every car that switches to a bike, 19 more bikes can ride the roads without adding more congestion.

Transport & Travel

BUT...

While riding a bike has major benefits, the main reasons that transportation continues to affect global warming won't be changed by bike riding in its current incarnation.

■ Even if everyone rode bikes, a large portion of transportation is shipping and long- distance travel, which would be unaffected. Consider this statistic published by the Environmental Defense Fund: If people who live within 5 miles (8 kilometers) of their workplace were to cycle to work just one day a week and leave the car at home, nearly 5 million tons of global warming pollution would be saved every year.[2] That is, if everyone in the whole of the United States participated (which is unrealistic), you would only save less than 1 percent of worldwide CO_2 emissions. This is because the majority of people live too far away from their jobs to bike.

■ Those calories still have to come from somewhere, and current agricultural practices—especially high-meat diets—contribute significant greenhouse gas emissions, so human power isn't greenhouse gas-free.

UPGRADE YOUR AUTOMOBILE?

YES...

Cars have been built to respond to a lot of different market pressures, and energy efficiency has been incorporated into cars since the late 1980s.

■ If you have an older car, then upgrading to a more modern car or a hybrid can give you a significant boost in fuel efficiency. Interestingly, some cars built between 1980 and 1985 or so actually got better gas mileage than even the best hybrid on the road today! It came, of course, at the expense of crash safety ratings, which weren't a major concern back then.

■ A new car features a more optimized engine with computer-controlled combustion, which results in much lower nitrogen oxide (NO_x) and particulate emissions.

■ If you're still driving a car left over from your parenting days, but now some of the children have gone away to school, upgrading to a smaller car can boost your fuel efficiency by cutting all the empty seats you're driving around.

BUT...

Overconsumption is a problem everywhere in modern life, so don't fall into the consumption trap with something as high-energy as a car.

■ When buying a new car, keep in mind the percentage increase in fuel efficiency: Most recent models are only 2–4 mpg different than their five-year-old counterparts. Going from 30 mpg to 36 mpg is only a 20 percent increase in efficiency. Compare that to a really significant rise, such as going from a 12 mpg SUV to the same 36 mpg sedan, a 66 percent increase. Try to find a car that does better than 40–50 mpg.

■ Additionally, the energy that goes into making a new car is high, and you will have to earn that energy back in fuel efficiency before you start making real gains compared to your last car. If the fuel efficiency is not significantly different, it may take forever to recoup the embodied energy of the car in fuel savings.

■ Finally, try altering your "passenger miles per gallon" rather than that of your car, by ride-sharing. Adding an extra person to a trip turns a 20 mpg ride into a very respectable 40 mpg ride, a 50 percent increase in fuel efficiency, and at a fraction of the cost.

Upgrade Your Automobile?

FILL UP WITH BIODIESEL?

YES...

Recently, colorful personalities have been in the news for driving around in cars that run on fuel made from old fryer oil, often joking, "My exhaust smells like doughnuts!" Despite their silliness, biodiesel, a fuel made from plant oils, is a very serious eco-opportunity.

■ If you have a diesel car, running it on biodiesel can help you reduce your emissions of nitrogen oxide and particulates, and produce 50 percent less smog-forming ozone.[1]

■ Because biodiesel is made from 100 percent plant oils, it has the potential to be largely carbon neutral (assuming that no fossil fuels are burned in its production or transport—a big assumption). And since biodiesel can be burned in existing cars and sold from existing pumps, this makes it a very enticing prospect as a replacement for petrodiesel.

■ Additionally, if, like the colorful characters mentioned earlier, you can source the oil for making your biodiesel from oil waste, then you are both eliminating a waste stream and getting your energy for "free," since it was already used once.

BUT...

Biodiesel is now big business, and its production has potential negative consequences for the environment.

■ Demand for biodiesel long outstripped the supply available, so now sunflower and soy are planted specifically to make oil for its production. In order to guarantee the highest yields possible, these crops are fertilized with fossil-fuel-based chemicals and processed with gasoline-burning equipment. According to a recent study, these inputs cause sunflower biodiesel to require 118 percent more fossil fuel than it produced, and soy biodiesel to require 27 percent more than it produced.[2] As net energy losers, we would be better off burning the fossil fuels.

■ Since biodiesel is made from food oils, its production has eaten into the agricultural production capacity for food, and in part, led to recent food shortages.

■ Increased demand means new lands are being used for soybeans, including land that was formerly covered with rainforest, in countries such as Brazil and Colombia, and marginal lands in developed countries that are better off being rested.

BUY GAS BLENDED WITH ETHANOL?

YES...

Shortly after we finished hearing about the wonders of biodiesel, politicians began trumpeting the praises of a new wonder fuel: ethanol. Actually, it isn't new—Henry Ford's Model T was originally designed to run on switchgrass ethanol. This old standard has plenty to recommend it.

■ Ethanol is made from fermented plant sugars, which are a renewable source of energy, so engines burning ethanol are potentially carbon neutral (assuming that no fossil fuels are used in production).

■ Unlike biodiesel, ethanol can be blended up to 85 percent with gasoline, and run in standard (non-diesel) engines with only minimal adjustment. Many cars sold in the United States and abroad already have this capability.

■ Like biodiesel, ethanol is reasonably portable and can be distributed via traditional gasoline infrastructure and gas stations (although less straightforward than gasoline). In many countries, E85, as it is known, is sold at the same pumps as gasoline.

BUT...

As with biodiesel, the size of the demand for liquid automotive fuels, and the compromises forced on ethanol production by business to meet that demand cheaply, have revealed an ugly side to ethanol.

WHAT TO DO
Don't count ethanol as a fuel alternative until a way is found to make cellulosic ethanol (made from plant waste rather than food) cost effectively.

■ The easiest way currently for North America to make ethanol is from corn. Corn causes soil degradation and fossil fuel reliance. According to a recent study, fossil fuel inputs cause corn ethanol to require 29 percent more fossil fuel than it produces. Other candidate plants, switchgrass and wood biomass, required 50 percent and 57 percent, respectively.[1] In other words, we would be better off burning the fossil fuels.

■ Since ethanol is made from corn, its production has eaten into the agricultural production capacity for food, and in part, led to recent food shortages. In 2007 Mexico suffered a corn shortage that led to increases in the price of tortillas of up to 50 percent in a few months.[2]

REDUCE YOUR AIR MILES?

YES...

Today many people think nothing of getting on a plane and flying hundreds or thousands of miles for a weekend trip. Flying is one of the most significant carbon-producing activities we take part in, so thinking about how we do it is key.

■ For the affluent consumers of industrialized countries, jet flights are a significant amount of individual carbon footprints, so reducing the number of flights you take is important. A single short-haul flight has one hundred times the warming effect of a similar-length drive in a two-passenger car.[1]

■ In addition, research indicates that greenhouse gas emissions and particulates released at high altitudes by planes may be more effective at causing global warming than ground-level emissions.

■ Unlike ground transportation, where low-carbon alternative fuels and hybrid drivetrains mean that cutting back on carbon doesn't have to mean cutting travel, there is no good low-carbon alternative for flying—except flying less.

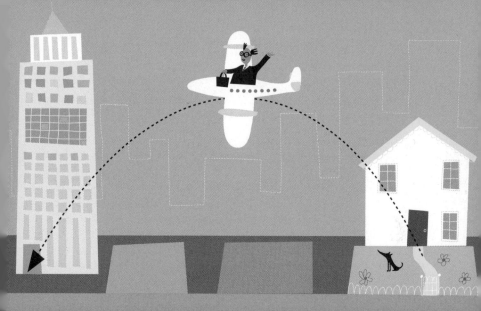

BUT...

Not all air miles are created equal. Generating fewer emissions on planes is a game of carefully considering what trips to make.

■ Because most emissions occur during takeoff and landing, short-hop flights actually have higher emissions per mile than longer flights—three times as many emissions, in fact.

■ When you think about taking alternative transport for a flight, consider the following: According to the Intergovernmental Panel on Climate Change, high-speed trains using coal-fired electricity (the case with many high-speed trains in Europe and Japan) are actually less efficient over distances from long-haul to almost medium-haul than planes. Similarly, someone driving a medium-haul distance alone in a small car might be comparable to a plane. If that person then loaded the car with boxes of supplies, it might tip the balance in the direction of flying.

CHAPTER FIVE

AT WORK

Though we call it "work," and talk about working in order to live, we spend a remarkable amount of time—sometimes as much as 50 percent of waking hours—at our jobs. Consequently, the choices we make during the course of our working lives have a major impact on our relationship with the environment. Even something as simple as printing a memo becomes a monumental ecological event when you imagine billions of similar employees around the world printing similar documents. Taking the idea further, and imagining the hundreds of recycling plants and collection trucks that would have to run to make alternative recycled paper for that same operation, brings home the environmental ambiguity of choices made at such a large scale. Make no mistake, there are serious opportunities to reduce waste, save energy, and reduce toxins, but the choices that lead to these reductions may be tricky to figure out, costly to implement, or both.

AVOID PRINTING?

YES...

Despite the "paperless revolution" computers have brought us, desktop publishing has us printing more than ever, much of it for only very short-term use. The best solution to cut paper waste is to not make so much of it in the first place.

■ Making high-brightness white paper often requires toxic bleaches and virgin pulp. Chlorine bleach used in making paper results in the creation of polychlorinated biphenyls (PCBs), dioxin, and furans,[1] some of the most toxic substances known.

■ Printer paper—virgin or recycled—requires high energy and water inputs to make, so cutting back on usage cuts back on these expenditures.[2]

■ The paper industry also produces high volumes of greenhouse gases, both from methane produced by rotting waste products and because harvesting trees for pulp releases CO_2 and methane as the discarded branches and leaves decompose.

BUT...

Don't assume that paperless options are fully benign.

■ Digital storage of files, especially long-term storage, can use significant energy in the form of server energy and cooling costs.

■ While digital files don't take up any space aside from the infrastructure where they are stored, they do use energy every time you look at them on a computer.[3]

■ Burning small documents onto compact discs creates waste that isn't collected by most municipal recycling centers.

■ Low-cost "giveaway" thumb (flash) drives take significant energy to create, and most contain lead, other heavy metals, and flame retardants.

USE RECYCLED PAPER?

YES...

Probably the first eco-friendly thing you learned to do was recycle your newspapers or other papers around the house.

■ Paper made from virgin fibers comes as a result of either deforestation or large monocultures of fast-growing trees, neither of which is eco-friendly.

■ The process of beating the trees into pulp requires much more energy and water than if recycled paper is used, because its fibers are already separated. Industry studies have shown that 28–70 percent of energy can be saved by using pulp from old paper, rather than virgin tree fiber.[1]

■ Recycling paper closes a loop on a huge potential waste stream. In 2005, in the richest countries, the average paper usage was just over 500 pounds per person per year.[2] This is organic waste that will eventually rot into methane greenhouse gas in landfills.

At Work

BUT...

While paper recycling is an important way to reduce waste and save energy, it's not a perfect environmentally friendly solution by any means.

■ Recycling paper made from wood pulp is a chemical-intensive process that results in the production of PCBs. Additionally, dioxin and furans are present in sludge wastes of the recycling process, which must then be disposed of.

■ Buying recycled paper sustains the demand for traditional wood-based paper, because paper fibers can be recycled five to seven times. Each time they become smaller, requiring new, longer fibers to be introduced. These longer fibers come from virgin pulp, which comes from trees, extending the supply but reducing the resource.

■ Higher-priced recycled paper perpetuates the market dominance of wood-fiber over alternative-fiber papers such as hemp and kenaf. Most purchasers see a choice between eco-friendly paper (high priced) and conventional paper (lower priced). These fibers require fewer harsh chemicals in their processing and produce less waste[4] but remain expensive largely because of limited availability due to low market demand.

Use Recycled Paper?

TELECOMMUTE TO WORK?

YES...

One of the greatest environmental potentials of computers and communication technology is the opportunity to spend less energy moving people from place to place, just so they can talk to one another.

■ If your office allows telecommuting, by all means take advantage of this. Cutting out one or two days of commute can save a huge amount of fuel, and benefit your own free time. In the United Kingdom, British Telecom estimates that its employees save over twelve million liters (about 3.2 million gallons) of fuel by working flexibly.[1]

■ Don't restrict telecommutes to everyday commuting. Saving one overseas business flight is the equivalent of a few months of commuting. Teleconferencing systems have become very advanced and are worth looking into.

■ Flexible working can also mean working fewer, longer days, which still cuts down total car trips, and can boost productivity by reducing the number of transitional times during a work day.

BUT...

Regardless of your scheduled relationship with your office, the geographic relationship between home and office is just as crucial.

■ Don't use "I only go in to the office a few days a week" as an excuse to live miles from work. It doesn't matter how many times you drive, just how much you drive. Nonscheduled trips to the office can still add up to a significant amount of driving.

■ If you must live further from work (for financial reasons, perhaps), consider living close to public transport. The benefit here is twofold. If you generally take the bus to work, you will cut your carbon emissions and be less likely to pop back to the office on a whim, since bus schedules make it less convenient.

■ If you are close to work, then it makes perfect sense to walk or cycle.

USE A REUSABLE COFFEE CUP?

YES...

For many of us, the day doesn't start without a cup of coffee—and it often doesn't stop with just one cup. When you consider this adds up to hundreds of cups per year, it becomes obvious that cup choice has significant potential for eco-impact.

■ When you reuse a coffee cup, you keep tons of waste out of landfills. Food and other packaging waste is a huge part of our waste stream—one that the European Union and various countries are actively trying to cut.

■ Reusing a cup also keeps the paper industry from producing the toxins associated with manufacturing one. Or, if it's a foam cup, reusing it keeps tiny floating bits of plastic from being eaten by sea animals and birds, putting added strain on food chains and ecosystems.

■ Finally, you avoid the greenhouse gas emissions from the drilling of oil to produce a plastic cup, or the cutting down of forest to produce a paper one.

At Work

BUT...

Depending on what you mean by "reuse a cup," things may not be as cut and dried as you expect.

■ Ceramic cups take more energy (and therefore petrochemicals) to make than polystyrene or paper alternatives. You would need to reuse a ceramic mug a thousand times in order to get the same production energy-per-use that a plastic cup has.

■ Washing that ceramic cup uses much more water over its lifetime than a comparable disposable cup. Add that to the energy needed to heat the water during washing. Then you have to factor in the possibility of the ceramic cup being lost, broken, or upgraded.

WHAT TO DO

Your best option is to buy a used cup at a thrift store, and only wash it once every day. Use a well-filled dishwasher. Try to stay away from the "free cup to all new hires" gimmick, as few people are likely to keep the cup long enough.

Use a Reusable Coffee Cup?

USE A LAPTOP COMPUTER?

YES...

Computing is among the fastest-growing segments of the modern office's energy expenditures.

■ Choosing a laptop over a desktop can seriously reduce energy use of individual workstations. Laptops use between a half and a quarter the power of desktops, especially desktops with separate cathode ray tube (CRT) monitors.

■ Computers are also a serious source of heat, which has to be removed by air conditioning during the summer. Air conditioning uses electrical power, and is much less efficient than heating, so it generates significantly more greenhouse gases. Computers that use less energy will generate less heat, cutting cooling expenditures.

> **WHAT TO DO**
>
> Unless you need the mobility, there are smaller, lower-energy desktop computers that can be upgraded very easily. Whatever computer you choose, keep it and repair it as long as you can.

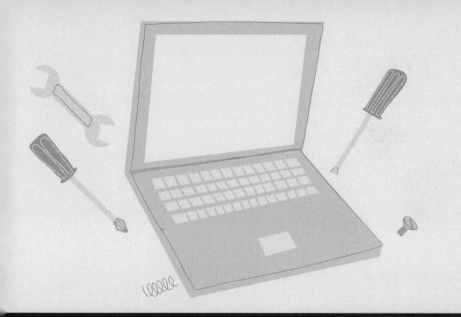

BUT...

Switching over to laptops just for energy savings may hide another significant environmental impact of these devices: waste.

■ Laptops are designed for portability and therefore have highly compact, integrated parts. Desktop computers are much more open inside, allowing users to upgrade and get broken parts repaired. Laptops, however, are largely not user-serviceable, which can lead to greater amounts of electronic waste. This highly toxic waste is a growing concern worldwide because it is difficult to dispose of or recycle safely.

■ Laptop parts are exposed to more harsh conditions—higher heat, vibration, and voltage fluxuations—over their lifetimes. This may lead to parts failing more quickly than in desktop systems.

■ Giving employees laptops may encourage them to take extra work home, which, while helpful in terms of productivity, increases total energy usage by the overtime spent using them at home.

GET CERTIFIED?

YES...

Often, companies aren't sure where to begin when it comes to optimizing their practices or office space to minimize their ecological impact—understandable, given the innumerable complexities of operating a business. In this case, getting an outside expert to help can be more effective and easier than figuring it out on your own.

■ In the United States, Leadership in Energy and Environmental Design (LEED) certification looks at the way your building, grounds, and some interior furnishings affect the environment, both from an ecological point of view and from a human perspective—eliminating volatile organic compounds (VOCs) from paint, for example, to avoid "sick building syndrome." Certification can also be sought for renovations on existing structures. All of this efficiency can be good for the business in terms of energy costs.

■ ISO 14000 is a set of guidelines that looks at the way your business practices affect the environment in the United Kingdom. This can involve everything from reducing paper use through digital workflows, and encouraging waste recycling programs, to implementing flexible working arrangements with employees.

BUT...

Certification is just a framework, nothing more. Just as with product certification, this is no excuse to be less informed about the decisions you are making. It's important that you be able to use the guidance of the framework, but know when recommendations are in line with your goals.

■ LEED is a great standard that is constantly evolving, but the implementation of different levels—gold, silver, platinum—has led to architects and planners stacking on extra points just to get a level boost, whether or not they actually benefit the environment or the company.

■ For example, a hotel in Las Vegas was recently certified as the largest LEED building in the world, with over 3,000 rooms and tens of thousands of square feet of additional conference room space.[1] This is in spite of the fact that Las Vegas is in the middle of the biggest drought in perhaps 500 years, primarily due to minimal water supplies in the first place, and a dramatically rising population, driven by the gambling and hotel industry.[2]

CHAPTER SIX

AT HOME

Our homes are the places that most reflect our goals and aspirations. Just as our first rooms are postered and painted to match our adolescent selves, when we grow up, we decorate our homes with evidence of our goals and values. This is a wonderful thing, since we spend so much of our lives in our homes; changes made there affect our lives in ways that few other places do. This also makes the home one of the best places to make changes to affect our ecological relationships. Most of our garbage, a large amount of our electricity, and the bulk of our appliances and devices reside in, flow through, or are discharged from our homes. However, since our homes are such nexus points for the different aspects of our ecological footprints, change in one has unique potential to become change in another—both for good and for bad. Careful consideration of what you gain and give up with each choice is essential when dealing with decisions that are so close to home.

BUY BAMBOO PRODUCTS?

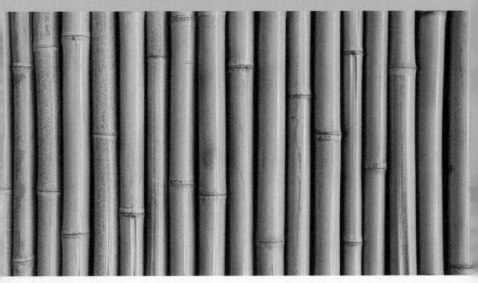

YES...

Bamboo has become a rising star among materials favored for being eco-friendly. Modern manufacturing turns this beautiful and useful grass into almost anything we can dream of.

■ Bamboo is an extremely fast-growing plant—some species can grow 12–19 inches per day.[1] At this rate, stocks can quickly be renewed, avoiding problems such as deforestation and soil loss (in the case of bamboo fiber products).

■ Bamboo has an extensive root system, which helps to stabilize hillsides on which it is grown, even when groves are continually harvested.[1] This helps alleviate erosion and watershed pollution due to excessive silt, which is a common side effect of traditional timber-based forestry.

■ Most bamboo being processed and sold is plantation grown, since consistency and quality is easier to obtain in this way. As a result, bamboo does not contribute to rainforest degradation. One study found that bamboo was a more eco-friendly choice than tropical hardwoods, metals, and plastics for furniture and utensils.[2]

BUT...

There is a big difference between a culm of bamboo in the woods and a roomful of bamboo flooring, or a bedspread of bamboo cloth.

■ Bamboo grows best in tropical environments, where the bulk of its production takes place. Most of the plantations supplying bamboo products sold in the United States, United Kingdom, and Europe are located in Thailand and southern China,[1] with high shipping costs for the fuel needed to transport it.

■ Since bamboo is a grass, its trunk is hollow, so even the biggest "lumber" is only around half an inch thick. The solution to this problem is to glue many smaller pieces of bamboo together. Many high-performance glues emit formaldehyde (a carcinogenic chemical) as they cure, which can result in months or years of "off-gassing" this chemical into people's homes.

■ Bamboo used in making textiles must be processed extensively using caustic chemicals including sodium hydroxide and sulfuric acid.[3] While it is safe if disposed of in a controlled manner, careless disposal has serious environmental consequences.

USE A DISHWASHER?

YES...

Dishwashers not only save time, but they can also save large amounts of water if used correctly.

■ Newer dishwashers use between 7–12 gallons (26–45 liters) of water per load of dishes, but according to the American Water Works Association, hand-washing can use as much as 20 gallons (75 liters). That could mean up to 13 gallons of water savings per dishwasher load.[1]

■ You can cut your water use by an additional 3–6 gallons (11–23 liters) per load[2] if you upgrade to a newer, more efficient dishwasher.

WHAT TO DO

Your best option is to wash your dishes in a fully-loaded European- or Japanese-manufactured washer—which conforms to high standards of water efficiency, and therefore uses less energy and water per load than other models. When hand-washing, use Castile soap (a mild vegetable soap) and use the rinse water on houseplants.

BUT...

Depending on how you use it, a dishwasher can also be an easy way to rack up additional water usage without even thinking about it.

■ If you're cleaning home pieces quickly before guests arrive, or if you live alone and don't want dishes sitting unwashed, and you've been tempted to fill the dishwasher only part way, remember that this uses the same amount of water as a full load. Since hand-washing uses a certain amount of water per item, washing fewer items means using less water. So, in the case of a very small load of dishes and a larger dishwasher, hand-washing is probably better.

■ If you aren't satisfied with your dishwasher's ability to clean off food unless you pre-rinse, you may as well just wash the dishes by hand. Pre-rinsing dishes before putting them in the dishwasher uses up to 20 additional gallons (76 liters) of water per load, according to the Colorado River Authority[2]—that's as much as hand-washing, plus whatever the dishwasher adds.

BUILD A NEW HOUSE?

YES...

Building a new house is a huge opportunity for making positive ecological choices; everything from materials, to the siting of the building, to electrical and heating systems within the house are subject to different options.

■ New construction lets you locate the house for optimal orientation with respect to the sun and prevailing winds for winter heating and summer cooling. Two studies performed in California found that home orientation could reduce winter heating costs by 10–20 percent and summer cooling costs by 10–40 percent.[1]

■ New construction allows you to think about passive heating and cooling principles, such as locating bedrooms in a position to create maximum time to cool by nighttime during the summer. Large building masses such as stone floors or brick walls can be positioned correctly for optimal heating and cooling performance.[2]

■ Building new also gives greater control over all the materials that go into a house. You have the chance to find alternatives for fiberglass insulation, which can cause lung problems as it ages, or to use formaldehyde-free plywood for floors and cabinets.

BUT...

New buildings can have serious environmental drawbacks also, especially when you shift your focus from the energy efficiency of a single house and begin to look at the efficiency of a community.

■ If you're building new, you are putting a lot of energy into a new building when there may be existing structures that can be retrofitted at similar or lower cost to have greater performance. Simple things such as adding double-paned glazing and insulation in an attic can have dramatic impacts on energy efficiency.

■ Building a new home from scratch typically generates much more waste than a renovation, and has the potential for greater damage to soil and local water quality because of concrete chemical runoff and other nonpoint source pollution.[3]

■ By renovating an existing building, you help strengthen a community, and the development of dense residential housing, rather than adding to urban sprawl. You can reduce commuting time, congestion, and the need for developed space, which can encourage preservation of wilderness spaces and greenways.

USE "NATURAL" CLEANING PRODUCTS?

YES...

Regardless of how modern and well heeled we are in our eco-shopping, the romantic notion of getting "back to nature" still carries some allure. Products with non-synthetic, "natural" ingredients appeal to that sensibility.

■ These products are less likely to contain derivatives of coal tar and petroleum, which have been shown to cause health problems, including cancers, in laboratory test animals, and which also support continued oil drilling and exploration.

■ These products are less likely to contain well-known offenders such as chlorine bleach and ammonia, which are implicated as asthma triggers.[1]

■ These products are also more likely to be made from renewable resources, such as soybeans, fruit peels, coconut, or timber waste. That can cut down on the ecological impact of their manufacture.

At Home

BUT...

Even without processing, nature is full of toxic chemicals, and the truth is that what you think means "natural" may not be what a manufacturer thinks it means.

■ Even totally natural chemicals can be extremely toxic—think about copper salts, arsenic, and lead. More realistically though, many naturally occurring compounds such as plant oils, pollen, and proteins can cause allergic reactions or trigger asthma—think about what peanut or coconut oil can do to certain people.

■ The cleaning products industry is largely unregulated, so unless the label contains a list of all the chemical components, then there is little guarantee that "natural" on the label means no petroleum chemicals in the bottle. Even an ingredient such as "coconut-derived surfactant" can contain petrochemicals and still be called "natural."[1]

■ Carcinogens are not tested for and may be present without the manufacturer's knowledge. The Organic Consumers Association in the United States sued the makers of nearly one hundred products for using the USDA organic label, because they contained known carcinogen 1.4-dioxane, in many cases without the manufacturer's knowledge.[2]

USE A WATER FILTER?

YES...

The bottled water industry has grown at a huge pace—2 percent per year on average.[1] All that extra work for the same water adds up to a heavy environmental cost.

■ Bottled water contributes a huge amount of plastic waste to the global stream every year. Between 1997 and 2005, US plastic-bottle production nearly quadrupled from 3.3 billion to 15 billion bottles annually.[2] Growth has been similar since, but recycling has been slow to catch up.

■ Shipping water around the world incurs a major energy cost. This translates into serious greenhouse gas emissions—as much as 0.25 kilograms (0.5 pounds) per bottle for water shipped from tiny tropical islands, and slightly less for more local water.[3]

■ Bottled water is up to 10,000 times as expensive as municipal water and, in many cases, of similar quality. If eco-friendly consumers can afford this extra expense, imagine the ecological benefit that could be realized with that amount of money, if it were put to a better use.

BUT...

Just because a filter is smaller than a mound of bottles doesn't mean it is impact-free.

■ There is still significant energy involved in making activated charcoal and resins for filters. Making charcoal involves burning coal or other carbonaceous materials in the presence of oxygen, which releases greenhouse gases.[4] There is waste associated with the disposable parts of filters, the shipping of the filters and associated products, and the packaging for sale in stores.

■ In most cases the quality of bottled water, or water produced by home filters is no different than the quality of water in your tap. Tap water may in fact be higher quality, as processing standards may be higher. The US Food and Drug Administration (FDA) assigns requirements for the purity of bottled water, based on the Environmental Protection Agency (EPA) requirements for the purity of municipal tap water.[2]

> **WHAT TO DO**
> Tap water is the lowest energy and waste option, so use it when you can. If, however, you have lead pipes, or iron-rich water, a water filter will keep things safe and tasty without the waste of bottles.

YES...

■ Washing clothes at lower temperatures saves significant energy, since you don't have to heat the water for the wash. Around 90 percent of the energy used to wash a load of clothes goes into heating the water for the wash.[1]

■ Modern detergents are formulated to work at lower temperatures, so there is no need for boiling water to clean clothes.

■ In modern societies, most clothes are worn only a few times before they are washed, so they don't need such hot water to cut through worn-in dirt on the clothing.

WASH AT 10°C LOWER
HOW MUCH ENERGY IS REALLY SAVED?

■ 20°C	120kW	70 joules
■ 30°C	240kW	140 joules
■ 40°C	360kW	210 joules
■ 50°C	480kW	280 joules
■ 60°C	600kW	350 joules

BUT...

While low-temperature washing has serious energy and greenhouse gas benefits, it has some problems in other areas.

■ Low-temperature washing does not kill headlice and bacteria. Temperatures of at least 50°C (122°F) are required to kill head lice in water.[2] With cooler water all you get is very clean headlice and bacteria.

■ In order to increase the effectiveness of detergents at low temperatures, manufacturers add chemicals such as tetra acetyl ethylene diamine (TAED), which are then released into the water system. This particular chemical has been linked to contact dermatitis.[3]

■ Manufacturers also add optical brighteners like phosphates to "make whites whiter," which can lead to algal blooms and fish death in streams after the water is flushed, and contact dermatitis in humans who wear the clothing.

CHAPTER SEVEN

DISPOSAL & RECYCLING

While there are now plenty of other problems that threaten humanity's comfortable structure of support from nature—global warming, durable toxic substances, and overfishing, to name a few—waste is definitely the oldest. Humans have probably made ecologically detrimental waste since before the invention of agriculture. Yet, tens of thousands of years later, we still throw away many times our own weight in garbage every year. In addressing the problem of waste we will have to look at three areas: amount, longevity, and toxicity. Unfortunately, it is rarely possible to reduce all of these parameters at the same time—and often, when this is possible, it is only at an economic cost. Recycling may reduce waste but produce toxins, or encourage more ubiquitous use of a material, generating more waste in the end. Composting may reduce one waste product, only to make more of another. In the end, the only sure bet may be to concentrate on making less waste in general—any other choice should be weighed carefully.

YES...

Plastic waste is a huge problem—arguably the biggest waste problem we face—so compostable alternatives are a boon to the mother throwing a birthday party for fifteen children, with all those plates.

■ Disposable cups, plates, and tableware make up a huge amount of annual waste, so choosing alternatives can help to cut down significantly on the waste that ends up destined for the landfill.

■ Tableware and dishes made from bamboo, bagasse (sugarcane pulp), potato starch, or plant-based plastics such as polylactic acid[1] (PLA) decompose naturally when exposed to oxygen and microorganisms.

WHAT TO DO

Avoid disposables altogether! Keep a ceramic or reusable plastic bowl at the office, and bring lunches in a metal tiffin lunch box or reusable plastic or wood bento box. If biodegradables are offered, make sure that there is a collection bin for composting.

BUT...

Biodegradability is complicated. It is dependent as much on the context that waste is left in as on the composition of the waste. Because of this, simply choosing biodegradable utensils may not generate the results you want.

■ Most municipal waste management strategies only incorporate a limited amount of composting infrastructure—the bulk of waste goes to incinerators or landfills. This either means that your carefully constructed plate burns just like a paper one, or in the case of a landfill, the lack of oxygen under all those layers of garbage and clay preserves your biodegradable plate just as well as a plastic one.[2]

■ If that weren't enough, biodegradable plastics are made from either corn or potatoes. When demand increases for these types of products, it eats into supply for the food market. Just as recently this has happened with corn-based ethanol, similar food price increases may result from increased adoption of these alternative plastics.

YES...

Despite your best culinary efforts to stretch your groceries, there will inevitably be bits and trimmings left over, and over time they can add up to a significant amount of waste. On top of that, a yearly tidying up of the garden will increase that waste pile by several times.

■ Composting your own yard waste and kitchen trimmings is a great way to keep it out of the landfill. According to the EPA, up to 24 percent of the average American's home waste is yard trimmings or food waste.[1]

WHAT TO DO

If you have twigs, sticks, or other woody yard clippings, try burning them as a substitute for charcoal in your outdoor barbecue or fire pit. If your town composts waste, they may capture methane for power generation. If not, careful turning of backyard compost can mostly eliminate methane production.

■ Compost is a valuable source of nitrogen and trace minerals, which your garden plants remove from the ground by growing. Making your own compost can return some of these nutrients for a healthier garden.

BUT...

What home composting benefits in waste, it makes up for in its potential for other serious environmental effects.

■ The bacteria responsible for digesting your compost release significant amounts of methane, a greenhouse gas twenty-one times as powerful as CO_2. If you aren't careful with turning your compost, you may switch what is primarily an aerobic reaction (high oxygen, CO_2-producing) to an anaerobic reaction (low oxygen, producing methane).[2]

■ The nutrient-rich liquids that leach out of home compost bins can be carried by rain into storm drains, and, like agricultural runoff, create algae blooms that rob streams of oxygen and kill fish. Proper siting and maintenance is needed to minimize this danger.

■ Perhaps most important, home composting takes feedstock material away from potentially carbon-neutral energy sources such as biogas fermenters. Without a municipal waste stream of organic matter (which is usually free, a considerable economic incentive), it's unlikely that these kinds of power sources will be developed

RECYCLE PLASTICS?

YES...

Plastic waste is a huge and growing problem that shows no sign of getting better any time soon. Measures to reduce it are an important part of being eco-conscious.

■ Recycling plastics reduces the amount of these long-lived materials that end up in landfills. The lifespan of a plastic bottle is hundreds of years in direct sunlight, and many times that in a landfill.

■ Recycling plastics reduces the prevalence of wind-blown trash such as bags and bottles, which can be mistaken by birds or other animals as food.

■ Most importantly, because plastic photodegrades, recycling reduces the amounts of ever smaller particles of plastic that eventually wash out to sea and are mistaken by fish as plankton, disrupting entire food chains, and resulting in crashes in population.

BUT..

Plastics are notorious for being downcycled—recycled into items of lesser value.

■ High-quality plastics such as the polyethylene terephthalate (PETE) used in soda bottles are almost never recycled into more soda bottles. The first-ever plant capable of producing "closed loop" food-grade plastic flake and pellets from municipal recycling came online in June 2008, and may still be the only one in the world.[1]

■ Instead, recycled plastics are generally made into low-performance items such as plastic lumber, parking lot speed bumps, or carpeting. These items are, in turn, almost never recycled, resulting in, at best, an extension of the utility of the original resource, but by no means making it sustainable.[2]

■ Even when plastics can be recycled into high-function products, they are often mixed with virgin resin, because the process of recycling degrades their properties significantly. Fifty percent resin is used in plastic; otherwise, the soda bottles mentioned above would be too weak.[1] All this encourages the continued use of petroleum and natural gas for plastics manufacture.

RECYCLE METALS?

YES...

Metals are some of the most energy-intensive materials from which we make things, and recycling can put a serious dent in this energy requirement.

■ Making metal from ore is always more energy intensive than starting from metal scrap. The difference varies depending on the type of metal, from iron, which is relatively easy to extract from ore, to aluminum, which requires ten times more energy to produce from ore than it does from cans. That means throwing an aluminum can away wastes energy equivalent to filling it halfway with gasoline and pouring it down the drain.[1]

■ Making metal from scrap also eliminates that much mining for ore, and the ecological damage that results. Mining for metal ores is responsible for environmental effects ranging from arsenic leaching into groundwater in Bangladesh, to rainforest deforestation, through bauxite mining in South America.

BUT...

Recycling doesn't undo the ecological impacts of choosing metal products.

■ Metals still require a huge amount of energy per use, recycled or not. For long-term-use items such as tableware or bicycles, this huge amount of initial energy might be worth it. But aluminum soda cans are used for minutes, and require a half a can of gasoline to make from scratch, so this energy use can be excessive.

■ Recycling metals such as iron and steel is basically like making them from ore, and requires the use of coal- or natural gas-fired furnaces, releasing significant greenhouse gas.

WHAT TO DO

Avoid short-life objects that use metals. Consider getting a draft pint at a pub rather than a canned beer. Eat fresh vegetables if possible, or even frozen since they have more nutritional value and generate less packaging waste. If you are a serious beer drinker, consider getting a kegerator system for your home. Kegs are reused many times by beer distributors. Making a keg requires much less energy than a comparable number of cans.

RECYCLE PAPER?

YES...

Paper is the original poster child of recycling—what could be more environmentally friendly than saving a tree?

■ Of course, there are other good reasons why paper gets such high marks. It takes the least energy of any material to get it from your curbside through the recycler and back into circulation. Additionally, recycling paper has huge energy savings of between 33–55 percent depending on the type of input paper and the desired output grade.[1]

■ Recycling paper also reduces the utilization of forest products, which can leave more land undisturbed. Every time a household recycles a year of daily papers, five trees are saved.[1]

■ Finally, recycling paper diverts massive amounts of waste from landfills or incinerators. In the European Union, over 35 percent of municipal waste is paper or cardboard from newspapers, bills, boxes, and other packaging supplies.[2]

BUT...

Recycling paper creates its own minefield of environmental issues, mostly to do with energy and waste.

■ Once used, paper is difficult to get clean and white again, and the bleaches and chemicals used to do this can create toxic chemicals such as PCBs, which can be flushed away in waste water and go on to pollute streams and waterways.[3]

WHAT TO DO
Recycling paper is an important waste reducer, but reducing total paper use to prevent waste is much more effective.

■ The sludge of ink and toner that washes from the recycled paper pulp contains a soup of nasty compounds, including dioxin and furans.[4] Proper disposal of this waste is crucial, but in some cases, it can escape into waterways or be put into inadequate landfills, where it can leach into groundwater.

USE CLOTH DIAPERS?

YES...

What could be a more obvious choice? Make mountains of waste, or reuse a few simple items?

■ Disposable diapers contribute a significant amount of waste to landfills—up to 2 percent in the United States.[1] Though this hasn't yet proven to be a problem, they also violate laws in most US states and many countries banning the disposal of untreated human waste in landfills.[2] In any case, they involve a significant amount of waste.

■ Some disposable diapers use plastic, a nonrenewable resource—up to 82,000 tons of plastic per year in the United States alone.

■ Some disposable diapers also use significant amounts of cellulose from trees. When compared to cotton diapers, they use up to seven times more raw materials to get the same utility as a reusable cloth diaper.[1]

BUT...

The diaper debate is by no means one sided. Cloth diapers, despite their soft appearance, have a heavy impact on the environment.

■ Cotton used in producing cloth diapers requires huge amounts of pesticides and results in serious degradation of soils.

■ Cloth diapers must be washed (but not necessarily a hot wash) to be reused, resulting in twice as much energy use per diaper change as a disposable, and almost half again as much water.[1]

■ Diaper laundering services also compound the problem, since they drive trucks on delivery routes, which do not benefit from the centralized distribution schemes that disposable diaper manufacturing enjoys.[1]

WHAT TO DO

Consider hybrid diapers, which have reusable cloth outers and toilet-flushable biodegradable inserts that absorb waste, letting you use one cloth outer a few times before washing. Also, potty train as soon as you can—for the environment, and your own sanity.

CHAPTER EIGHT

LIFESTYLE

Animals have instincts—genetically ingrained goals and behaviors—that tell them what to do and when to do it. Humans, on the other hand, have forsaken an instinctive past for something different: culture. The cultural heritage and traditions that we share with one another are a powerful part of what guides our actions. Another, more immediate, word for part of this cultural understanding is lifestyle. We adopt a lifestyle for ourselves after seeing it in others, or hearing it described. What makes the idea of *lifestyle* choices so powerful is that they can spread from person to person, almost like a disease; one year, you discover a cute purse at a local vendor, then it's being worn by the women in your office, then on national TV. The test that this puts to environmentally conscious individuals is this: What will you choose for yourself, knowing that others may follow? More important, would your choice be different if you knew that thousands of people would be making the same one?

WEAR ORGANIC COTTON?

YES...

Though mention of the word "*cotton*" conjures up all sorts of pastoral scenes and puffy-cloud daydreams, the reality of this crop is much darker.

■ Cotton is one of the most chemical-intensive plants grown. Even in the United States, a country with relatively progressive agrochemical regulations, as much as 10 percent of agricultural chemicals used—pesticides, fertilizers, defoliants—are sprayed on cotton each year.[1]

■ Organic cotton reduces the use of pesticides through interplanting with trap crops that lure pests away from the cotton crop and toward beneficial insect predators that live on the other plants.[1]

■ Synthetic fertilizer use is eliminated by using natural soil amendments such as compost, and rotating cotton with other crops that fix nitrogen in the soil.[1]

BUT...

Organic cotton, like many eco-labeled products, can often hide problems behind its well-meaning facade.

■ Organic farming methods can cost more, especially when initially switching from conventional to organic, since it can take time to build up the synergies that help organic work without synthetic inputs. Higher costs make some manufacturers seek out cotton markets where labor costs are low, but transport distance increases greenhouse gas emissions.

■ Additionally, cotton cultivation is a heavily water-dependent crop, using large amounts of freshwater. While organic production cuts irrigation needs to some extent through improved soil composition, it is still a high user compared to other crops.

WHAT TO DO

Choose organic cotton grown nearby if possible, and take good care of clothes to reduce the total amount of cotton you need to buy.

WEAR NATURAL FIBERS?

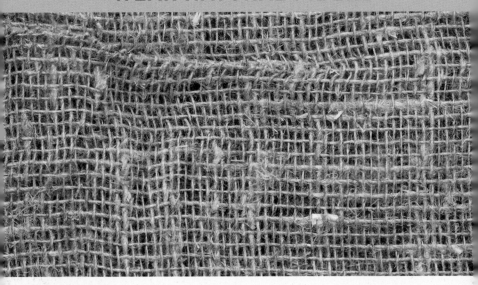

YES...

Again, that "natural" term comes into play, and again, there is some truth to the idea that natural fibers—that is, those from plants—are a better ecological choice.

■ Natural fibers such as cotton, wool, linen, hemp, and ramie can be made without the use of petroleum as a feedstock. In that sense, they are renewable in a way that synthetic fibers are not.

■ If grown organically, they need not use synthetic fertilizers or pesticides, so they don't result in the production of synthetic chemical pollutants such as synthetic fibers.

■ They are also generally more breathable and comfortable than synthetics, and when they wear out, they can safely biodegrade back into the soil, if composted properly.

BUT...

Despite their petroleum roots, synthetic fibers have a few things going for them as well.

■ Some synthetics, such as polyester or nylon, can be totally recycled into new garments at their end of life with similar energy input to processing from virgin materials.[1]

■ Some "natural" fibers, such as "bamboo" fiber, are really cellulose-based viscose made in processes that involve large amounts of heat to break down and dissolve the cellulose, using toxic chemicals such as sulfuric acid to solidify the spun cellulose fibers.

■ Finally, fiber-producing animals like sheep are often treated with pesticides to control insects and ward off disease, which can reduce fiber quality and introduce damaging compounds into the environment.

USE RECHARGEABLE BATTERIES?

YES...

Using rechargeable batteries is a great way to ease your electronic impact on the environment.

■ Disposable batteries represent a significant amount of material—between 400 and 800 times the material in rechargeables—since this is the range of recharges you can expect. (Although in practice, this may not be nearly so high.)

■ Alkaline batteries previously had mercury in their chemistry to improve performance. Major name brands have been working to eliminate mercury from batteries since the 1990s,[1] but low-cost batteries from overseas manufacturers may still contain significant amounts. With 800 alkalines for every rechargeable battery, this can add up to a lot of mercury used in production.

■ Alkaline batteries represent a significant amount of energy expenditure—even if you just look at shipping energy—without considering the energy needed to manufacture 800 cells versus one rechargeable cell.

Lifestyle

BUT...

For all the problems with alkaline batteries, rechargeables, especially low-cost ones, may have more environmental problems.

■ Nickel cadmium (NiCd) batteries contain high levels of cadmium, a metal that attacks many parts of the human body, including the kidneys and bones whenever ingested.

WHAT TO DO

Use rechargeable NiMH batteries, but be sure to dispose of them properly at special "household toxic waste" days held by your local municipality.

■ Newer nickel-metal hydride batteries (NiMH), while less dangerous, contain cobalt, a toxic metal that, like cadmium, can bioaccumulate in plants, resulting in toxic "hot spots" where batteries are made or disposed of incorrectly.

■ What may be even more dangerous is battery production. According to China's State Environmental Protection Agency, over 10 percent of China's arable land is contaminated with cadmium from sources such as battery and electronics factories—and the heavy metal has begun to enter the general population's food supply.[2]

YES...

If for no other reason than that they don't make items that could be termed waste (old photographs), your internal eco-meter might tell you that digital cameras are better for the earth than print.

■ Digital cameras use no chemicals to process photographs, while traditional print production uses a wide range of chemicals of varying toxicity, including hydroquinone, metol, borates, and ethylenediaminetetraacetic acid (EDTA). In common practice these chemicals are disposed of by diluting heavily with water and dumping in municipal drains, which leads to their introduction into stream ecosystems.

■ Digital cameras allow you to choose which photos you would like to expend resources on, only printing the ones you like.

BUT...

Although digital cameras don't seem to create waste, that doesn't mean that they don't have any environmental effects.

■ While the energy used to make a digital camera may be only slightly higher than that required to make a still camera of comparable materials, the energy required to constantly recharge batteries, or buy new ones, is significantly greater over the life of the camera.[1]

■ More important, though, a study by the Georgia Institute of Technology in the United States, found that enough energy was consumed by manipulation of photos on camera and computer screens to negate the energy expenditures in processing film.

WHAT TO DO

Camera for camera, either option has benefits that outweigh the other. Your best bet is to buy a durable camera (film or digital), use rechargeable batteries (if digital), and print only those pictures you want to keep (either to avoid processing chemicals or screen display energy).

PLANT A TREE?

YES...

If treehugging is the ultimate embodiment of being green, then what could be more eco-friendly than planting a tree?

■ Trees absorb CO_2 from the atmosphere and convert it into wood. This can theoretically mitigate greenhouse emissions from cars and fossil fuel energy. Hundreds of tree-planting concerns have spung up in the last decade just to sell carbon credits based on tree planting.

■ Trees stabilize soil and soak up water that might cause mudslides.

■ Trees provide a renewable resource for building. Wood is an exceptional material: Light, strong, and easily workable, it is an important part of the building of sustainable designs. Plus, while growing, this resource provides habitat for animals and cover for understory plants.

BUT...

While a beautiful symbol for the eco-movement, the planting of trees without regard to their environmental appropriateness is a recipe for problems.

■ According to Govindasamy Bala, an atmospheric scientist at the Lawrence Livermore Laboratory in California, only trees planted within the band of tropical forest around the equator (plus or minus 20 degrees latitude) are decreasing global warming. They evaporate water, which produces reflective clouds.[1]

■ Trees outside of that band absorb solar radiation and cause the air to warm. They can even negate the reflective effect of icy tundra by growing on top of it in latitudes above 50 degrees.[1]

■ Unless cut and preserved as wood, their carbon ends up rotting out in methane, or burning out in CO_2, re-releasing any greenhouse gas gains they eliminated.

■ Even reduced soil erosion may disrupt the iron cycle in oceans, where nutrient-rich soil dust blows in, and fertilizes phytoplankton, which grow, absorb CO_2, die, and carry that carbon into the deep ocean.

WEAR ECO-FRIENDLY SHOES?

YES...

Shoes are a major environmental headache from a number of perspectives. Shoe manufacturers have picked up on this and are offering new models with a variety of options to help you cut your "footprint."

■ Leather is tanned using heavy-metal salts, which produce wastewater that is extremely toxic to people and local ecosystems.

■ Because of the complex shapes of traditional shoe designs, shoe production results in a lot of waste. Most of it is not recyclable, toxic, or both.

■ Most shoes use liberal amounts of petrochemical-based glues, rubbers, and foams, which off-gas toxic chemicals as they dry, and release toxic chemicals as they wear.

■ All this means particularly bad things for manufacturing countries, which end up with toxic waste leaching from factories into water supplies and farmland, and exposure to high concentrations of toxic fumes from glues and foams.

BUT...

Shoes touted as eco-friendly may not be a perfect solution, especially depending on what "eco-friendly" means to that manufacturer.

■ In order to keep costs down, many eco-labeled shoes are still manufactured overseas, or great distances from where they are sold, making their carbon footprint similar to that of conventional shoes.

■ While vegetable-tanned leather is less toxic than chrome-tanned alternatives, it requires much more water, which may not be disposed of properly and can still be toxic to local streams.

■ In order to align themselves with vegan customers, many of these shoe manufacturers opt for fabric uppers instead of leather, which are not as durable as a leather shoe. Similarly, natural latex rubber is not as durable as high-quality synthetic rubber. If a pair of eco-friendly shoes lasts only a half or a third as long as a pair of conventional shoes, then they have to be that much more eco-friendly to compete.

YES...

If you are concerned that your vacation to a far-off land might have had a serious environmental impact, you would be right.

■ Long-distance air travel for vacationing results in 7 percent of global carbon emissions each year.[1] So, staying close to home can mean big carbon savings—even 12,000 miles of driving releases less CO_2 than a single transatlantic round-trip.[2]

■ In addition to that, alternative modes of long-distance vacationing—such as cruises—can damage coral reefs and spread pollution, which can lead to disruption of food chains and loss of biodiversity.

■ By camping in wilderness areas or state or national parks near your home, you are more aware of your local ecology and watershed and whether they are in good shape. Being better informed should help you and your neighbors vote for the environmental reforms that help keep these natural resources healthy for future generations.

BUT...

Tourism—greenhouse gas emissions aside—is a powerful ecological force throughout the world, and one not to be given up lightly.

■ Tourists naturally gravitate to the beautiful areas of the world: rainforests, coral reefs, and pristine sandy beaches. Tourism dollars are a major incentive for local populations of people to develop rules and strategies for caring for these resources so that they will continue to bring in tourists, and their money. That's one of the major economic engines that fuels conservation.

■ Many ecologically pristine areas adjoin areas with significant populations of people who make their livelihood based on tourist dollars. If fewer tourists visit these areas, then these people will be forced to find new ways of making a living. This may lead to unintentional degradation of ecosystems through increased farming on marginal land. It may also cause intentional degradation of ecosystems through poaching of protected species, or illegal logging of old growth.

BOOK A VACATION AT AN ECO-RESORT?

YES...

So, you've decided to visit an eco-resort in a place such as Fiji, and you figure that:

■ These earth-conscious destinations often feature on-site power generation through solar or wind, locally grown food, and minimalist structures built on stilts or other ways that do not disturb their pristine surroundings.

WHAT TO DO

If you do go on vacation in well-traveled tourist traps, consider an eco-resort for its low impact. But, give pristine areas a break—avoid vacations there.

■ Vacations often include guided tours of virgin rainforest, or coral reefs, giving visitors a perspective on these ecosystems difficult to get any other way. This perspective can be a great way to help visitors make hard choices to preserve these environments.

■ Perhaps most important, these resorts give local people income that does not require them to clear rainforest for farming.

BUT...

The most damaging part of tourism is, in the end, the tourists themselves. No matter how well designed a resort is, or how much of its own energy it creates, human presence has an inevitable impact on all ecosystems, especially pristine ones.

■ These resorts are often built on remote islands or coastal areas whose ecosystems are not durable enough to withstand constant human habitation.

■ In addition to using local food and water supplies, human visitors bring diseases to native animals and seeds of invasive plants that put extra strain on already fragile areas.

■ Being remotely located, these resorts require larger amounts of air travel, with multiple takeoffs and landings, the most carbon-intensive parts of a flight.

■ Finally, because many of these resorts are owned by non-native companies, the amount of money that stays in local economies is not necessarily large. In fact, locals may be making less than in conventional tourist locations because the resort's remote location, away from other competition, allows it to control wages.

BUY CARBON OFFSETS?

YES...

In our modern fossil-fueled world, some carbon emissions are inevitable, particularly as technologies are developed and infrastructure changed to allow for purchase of carbon-free energy.

■ Buying offsets that fund the planting of trees or the preservation of rainforest land not only absorbs carbon from the atmosphere, but also promotes the well-being and creation of wildlife habitat.

■ Buying offsets that fund businesses to upgrade their manufacturing infrastructure for greater energy or carbon efficiency also improves future industrial emissions.

> **WHAT TO DO**
>
> Buy offsets only as a last resort. Reduce everything you can through real action on your part, and if you are interested in offsets, research the provider thoroughly to ensure that your money isn't better spent elsewhere.

■ Buying offsets that fund the creation of alternative power such as wind farms and solar infrastructure also helps make carbon-free power available to everyone.

BUT...

Although offsets seem valid in principle, their actual capacity for reducing carbon emissions is much less clear.

■ In a study carried out by UK research group Environmental Data Services in 2008, out of 170 companies selling carbon offsets, only 30 were found to provide "high quality"—environmentally effective—offsets.[1]

■ Biomass planting schemes have questionable effectiveness in reducing carbon because companies may not stay in business long enough to ensure that biomass is protected, and tree planting, as mentioned earlier, is not clearly effective.

■ Lax regulation in voluntary markets leads to poorly defined, and even fraudulent, credits, according to the US Federal Trade Commission (FTC).[2]

WHAT NEXT?

By now, you've seen how some questions that seem cut and dried can get very difficult to sort out. This book is by no means an exhaustive list of examples, and even the most extensive list of examples would become outdated in seconds at the rate that new understanding, new technology, and new crises are developing. Examples like toxic BPA (bisphenol A) in polycarbonate water bottles (intended as a substitute to counteract the waste of disposable water bottles) show just how easy it is for one problem to become another if not considered from many angles.

You've already read one book to get more informed about eco-choices. Don't make it your last. Find out about your world. Ask your grocer where your food comes from. Ask your pharmacist how your drugs are made. Ask the desk clerk at the hardware store where their brooms are manufactured. Ask your neighbors how much they pay during the winter to heat their houses, and why they pay less, if they do. Ask your grandparents how they used to buy and use clothes, and how they repaired them. Read newspapers and magazines, and if a story seems ridiculous, or too good to be true, ask yourself how you can check online or with a librarian to see if the facts support the story. If they don't support the story, ask yourself what the story should be, and tell someone about it.

If you've got good information about the issues, then you are well informed enough to make these decisions. Unfortunately, getting all the information can take too much precious time, so, in a pinch, try these suggestions out, but make sure you agree that they are valid before you treat them as rules.

• Make the choice that uses the least fossil fuels per use. Maybe this means an item uses a lot of renewable energy, or just a little fossil fuel. Maybe it lasts a long time, so the energy gets spread out over many uses.

• Make the choice that makes your local community and ecosystem more resilient. Maybe this means planting a vegetable garden, or planting native plants instead of grass. Maybe it means volunteering with a youth group or cleaning up a stream. Or maybe it means buying products made locally, or starting a business that services local needs.

• Make the choice that results in less durable, dangerous waste. Maybe this means saying no to coal power, buying bulk groceries, saying no to plastic, buying repairable shoes, or learning how to upgrade your computer.

In any case, make the choice that reflects as much as you know about the situation, and keep on reconsidering that choice as you get new information. Politicians and countries may decide the fate of large-scale things such as the Kyoto Accord, the Nuclear Nonproliferation Treaty, and international trade policies. But just as your votes decided which politicians had a say in those policies, the actions you take in your life will decide which traditions and norms are passed on to our children. Humans may not be necessary to save nature, but we certainly have an effect on how nature saves us. We can make it as easy, or as hard, as we like. The choice is ours.

WHAT IS A CARBON FOOTPRINT?

You may have heard that life on earth is "carbon based." What this means is, while life runs on energy from the sun, plants and animals store that energy and build their bodies with chemical compounds that contain carbon. This carbon cycles between carbon-based gases, such as CO_2 and methane, in the atmosphere, and carbon-based chemicals, such as sugars, cellulose, fats, and proteins, in the bodies of plants and animals. Carbon compounds in the earth's atmosphere—such as methane and CO_2—act as a reflective layer to infrared radiation from the earth's surface, trapping heat and keeping the earth warm. Global warming results when concentrations of these carbon compounds increase, and cooling results when concentrations are reduced. Normally, atmospheric carbon levels stay within a range that results in the climates that humans have adapted to live in around the world. Burning fossil fuels for the past 200 years has altered this balance and led to changes in climates from the Arctic to the equator.

In order to minimize the changes that worldwide climates will undergo, we need to get our carbon production under control, and the first step is to keep track of how much atmospheric carbon we release. Large entities such as countries and corporations are making inventories of the greenhouse gas emissions they make, and building markets and treaties around these numbers. But you don't have to be big to know your contribution. A carbon footprint is the amount of carbon that one individual's activities release into the atmosphere each year. These emissions can be from electrical power generation, driving a car, buying products that need to be shipped, growing vegetables using synthetic fertilizer, or heating a home. Carbon footprints are typically expressed in tons of CO_2 equivalent (one ton of methane gas has the equivalent warming capacity of 25 tons of CO_2). In this way, many different sources of carbon, such as burning fuel, making electricity, and farming, can all be compared evenly.

What Is a Carbon Footprint?

Calculating your carbon footprint by yourself can be a daunting prospect, considering that you need to take so many inputs into account. For this reason, many organizations have put together calculators that are available online. They ask for things such as the average distance you drive per month, where you live (since power generation using coal has different emissions than power generation using natural gas), how much you fly, how many showers you take, and other questions about energy usage. Finding the total amount of your carbon footprint is just the beginning; once you do, it's important to compare your number to averages from your country and other countries to get an idea of what your reduction goals might be. Since energy usage statistics vary from country to country, it is important that you find a calculator that is appropriate for yours. Here are a few providers of calculators and average usage statistics.

The US Environmental Protection Agency has a calculator at:
http://www.epa.gov/climatechange/emissions/ind_calculator.html

Or, for an alternate location, Berkeley has a calculator at:
http://coolclimate.berkeley.edu/

In the UK, DEFRA has a calculator at:
http://actonco2.direct.gov.uk/index.html

LIST OF RESOURCES

FOOD

Buy Organic?

1) World Health Organization, *Public Health Impact of Pesticides Used in Agriculture* (1990, WHO)

2) UN Economic and Social Council, *"Economic, Social and Cultural Rights,"* Commission on Human Rights, 58th session (2002)

3) UN Environment Programme, *Challenges to International Waters; Regional Assessments in a Global Perspective* (February 2006, UN)

4) Davis, Donald R., "Trade-Offs in Agriculture and Nutrition," *Food Technology* (Vol. 59, No. 3, 2005)

5) Ness, Carol, "Organic Label Muddies the Waters" *San Francisco Chronicle* (28 April 2004)

6) World Wildlife Fund, *Benchmarking Study of Organic Aquaculture Standards* (2007, WWF)

7) Fromartz, Samuel, "What Makes a Cow Organic?" *In Good Tilth Magazine* (Vol..18vi., 2008)

Buy Local?

1) Watkiss, Paul, *et al.*, "The Validity of Food Miles as an Indicator of Sustainable Development," *AEA Technology Environment Study for DEFRA* (July 2005)

2) Kwok, Roberta, "Is Local Food Really Miles Better?" *Salon* (24 June 2008)

Eat Less Meat?

1) Steinfeld, H. *et al.*, *"Livestock's Long Shadow: Environmental Issues and Options,"* Rome: UN (2006)

2) Bellows, B., "Managed Grazing in Riparian Areas," *National Center for Appropriate Technology* (2003)

3) Earl, J.M., "The Benefits of Increasing Defoliation Interval. Proc.," *Grassland Society of NSW* 12th Annual Conference (pp.143–145, 1997)

4) Silver, K., "Pink Gold," *Spirit Magazine* (2008)

5) Holt, Gordy, "Goats Provide Alternative to Chemicals for Weed Control," *Seattle Post Intelligencer* (August 2005)

Eat Less Corn?

1) Pollan, Michael, *The Omnivore's Dilemma : A Natural History of Four Meals* (2006, Penguin Press)

2) Pimentel, D., "Soil Erosion: A Food and Environmental Threat," *Environment, Development and Sustainability Journal* (Vol. 8, February 2006)

3) Pimentel, D., "Ethanol Fuels: Energy Balance, Economics, and Environmental Impacts Are Negative," *Natural Resources Research* (Vol. 12, 2003)

Eat Less Fish?

1) Issenberg, Sasha, *The Sushi Economy: Globalization & the Making of a Modern Delicacy* (2007, Gotham Books)

2) AIDA web site, "Shrimp Trawling Bycatch" (2007), http://tinyurl.com/55oy4w

3) Stier, Ken, "Fish Farming's Growing Dangers," *Time Magazine* (September 2007)

4) Brown, Lester, "Fish Farming May Soon Overtake Cattle Ranching as a Food Source," *Earth Policy Institute* (2001), http://tinyurl.com/5dtwvp

Grow Your Own Food?

1) Bormann, F. Herbert; Balmori, Diana; Geballe, Gordon T., *Redesigning the American Lawn* (1993, Yale University Press)

2) Ruff, Joshua, "Levittown, the Archetype for Suburban Development," *American History Magazine* (2008)

Say No to GMOs?

1) Stewart Jr, C. Neal; Richards IV, Harold A.; Halfhill, Mathew D., "Transgenic Plants and Biosafety: Science, Misconceptions and Public Perceptions," *BioTechniques* (October 2000)

2) Taylor, S.L., "Food from Genetically Modified Organisms and Potential for Food Allergy," *Environmental Toxicology and Pharmacology* (November 1997)

3) Pray, Carl E.; Huang, Jikun; Hu, Ruifa; Rozelle, Scott, "Five Years of BT Cotton in China: The Benefits Continue," *The Plant Journal* (Vol. 31, 2002)

SHOPPING

Consider "Embodied Energy"?
1) Harden, Blain, "Dirt in the New Machine," *New York Times Magazine* (12 August 2001)
2) Canadian Architect web site, "Embodied Energies of Common Building Materials," http://tinyurl.com/5pcvm
3) Cox, Billy, "Throwaway Society Speeds Decline of Electronics Repairmen," *USA Today* (1 January 2004)

Buy Certified Products?
1) Byers, Alice, *"Value-Adding Standards in the North American Food Market,"* United Nations FAO (2008)
2) Severson, Kim, "Suddenly, the Hunt Is on for Cage-Free Eggs," *New York Times* (12 August 2007)
3) Forest Stewardship Council, www.fsc-watch.org

Buy More Eco-Products?
1) European Communities Commission, *"Report to the Council & European Parliament on the Implementation of Directive 94/62/EC on Packaging and Packaging Waste and its Impact on the Environment,"* (12 June 2006)

Do Some Eco-Remodeling?
1) U.S. Department of Energy web site, "Tips for Saving Energy at Home," http://tinyurl.com/ytln8c
2) DeOreo, W. *et al.* *"Retrofit Realities,"* AWWA Journal (Vol. 93, Iss. 3, pp.58–72, March 2001)
3) EIONET web site, "What Is Waste?" *European Topic Centre on Resource and Waste Management*, http://tinyurl.com/5wgmuu

Use Paper Bags?
1) Lapidos, Juliet, "Will My Plastic Bag Still Be Here in 2507?" *Slate Magazine* (27 June 2007)
2) The Guardian web site, "Photoessay: Plastic Bags" (February 2008), http://tinyurl.com/348eoz
3) "Resource and Environmental Profile Analysis of Polyethylene and Unbleached Paper Grocery Sacks," *Franklin and Associates Inc.* (1990)
4) National Packing Covenant Council, "Plastic Shopping Bags in Australia," *Environment Protection and Heritage Council Report* (6 December 2002)
5) Ecobilan, "Évaluation des Impacts Environnementaux des Sacs de Caisse Carrefour. Analyse du Cycle de Vie de Sacs de Caisse en Plastique, Papier et Matériau biodégradable," *Carrefour Report* (February 2004)

Make Purchases Online?
1) Grist web site, Makower, Joel, "Ship It, Ship It Good" (May 2006), http://tinyurl.com/6nddpn

ENERGY

Use Clean Coal?
1) HowStuffWorks web site, Dowdey, Sarah, "What Is Clean Coal Technology?" (18 July 2007), http://tinyurl.com/4covyy
2) Shnayerson, M. *Coal River* (2008, Farrar, Straus and Giroux)
3) Johnson, Deryl B., *Centralia* (2004, Arcadia)
4) U.S. Environmental Protection Agency web site "Mercury Emissions—A Global Problem" (2004), http://tinyurl.com/6p2u8w

Generate Your Own Energy?
1) Toolbase web site, "Combined Heat and Power Systems for Residential Use," http://tinyurl.com/5vvy96
2) Energy Saving Trust web site, "Home Insulation and Glazing," http://tinyurl.com/5zp25g
3) U.S. Department of Energy web site, "Demand Tankless Water Heaters" (12 September 2005), http://tinyurl.com/6hxav7

Use Solar Energy at Home?
1) Bizzarri, G.; Morini, G.L., "A Life Cycle Analysis of Roof Integrated Photovoltaic Systems," *IJETM* (Vol. 7, No.1/2, pp.134–146, 2007)
2) Kharif, Olga, "Solar Cells: The New Light Fantastic," *Businessweek* (31 January 2005)

Choose Tidal Power?
1) U.K. Sustainable Development Commission, *Turning the Tide: Tidal Power in the U.K.* (1 October 2007, UKSDC)
2) Statkraft Energy Group, Norway, "Tidal Power, Versatile, Reliable, Renewable" (February 2006, SEG)
3) Kinver, Mark, "The Ebb and Flow of Tidal Power," *BBC News* (12 June 2008), http://tinyurl.com/5qgjt8
4) Environmental and Energy Study Institute, "Renewable Energy Factsheet" (May 2006)

Choose Hydroelectric Power?
1) Northwest Power Conservation Council web site "Dams' Effect on Salmon," http://tinyurl.com/6yq4t5
2) Duncan, Graham-Rowe, "Hydroelectric Power's Dirty Secret Revealed," *New Scientist* (February 2005)

TRANSPORT & TRAVEL

Drive a Hybrid?
1) HowStuffWorks web site, "How Hybrid Cars Work,"
http://tinyurl.com/5jxggf

Ride a Bike?
1) Whitelegg, John, *Transport for a Sustainable Future: The Case for Europe* (1993, Belhaven Press)
2) Environmental Defence Fund web site, "Bike Commuting Enjoys a Rebirth," http://tinyurl.com/6lhmra

Fill Up with Biodiesel?
1) Clean Air USA web site, "Biodiesel is Better for Your Lungs," http://tinyurl.com/6k952t
2) Pimentel, D.; Patzek, T.W., "Ethanol Production Using Corn, Switchgrass, and Wood; Biodiesel Production Using Soybean and Sunflower," *Natural Resources Research* (Vol. 14, pp.65–76, 2005)

Buy Gas Blended with Ethanol?
1) See citation 2, Fill Up with Biodiesel?
2) Roig-Franzia, Manuel, "A Culinary and Cultural Staple in Crisis," *Washington Post* (26 January 2006), http://tinyurl.com/yqp9wj

Reduce Your Air Miles?
1) Grid-Arendal, "Aviation and Global Atmosphere," *UNEP IPCC* (2001), http://tinyurl.com/5nwvwc

AT WORK

Avoid Printing?
1) Safe, Stephen H., "Polychlorinated Biphenyls (PCBs): Environmental Impact, Biochemical and Toxic Responses, and Implications for Risk Assessment," *Critical Reviews in Toxicology* (Vol. 24, pp.87–149, 1994)
2) Koay, J., *Environmental Impact of Paper Recycling* (1992, University of Manchester)
3) Fairfield, Hannah, "Pushing Paper Out the Door," *New York Times* (10 February 2008)

Use Recycled Paper?
1) Ogilvie, S.M., "A Review of the Environmental Impact of Recycling," *Warren Springs Lab., Stevenage* (1992)
2) See citation 3, Avoid Printing?
3) See citation 1, Avoid Printing?
4) ATTRA NCAT web site, Sullivan, Preston, "Kenaf Production" (2003), http://tinyurl.com/5u8yah

Telecommute to Work?
1) WorkWise U.K. web site, "Flexible Working: A Triple Win for People, Enterprise, and the Environment" (2006), http://tinyurl.com/6yawly

Get Certified?
1) "The Palazzo Las Vegas Named Largest 'Green' Building in the World," *Reuters* (10 April 2008) http://tinyurl.com/5aceka
2) Tanner, Adam, "Las Vegas' Growth Depends on Dwindling Water Supply," *Reuters* (21 August 2007), http://tinyurl.com/5qv2zl

AT HOME

Buy Bamboo Products?
1) Fu, Jinhe, "Moso Bamboo in China," *ABS Magazine* (Vol. 21, No.6, December 2000)
2) Van Der Lugt, Pablo, "Design Interventions for Stimulating Bamboo Commercialization," *VSSD Publications* (2008), http://tinyurl.com/6duako
3) Mindfully.org web site, Praveen Kumar Jangala; Haoming, Rong, "Making Rayon Fiber" (1999), http://tinyurl.com/5lt736

Use a Dishwasher?
1) AWWA web site, "Dishwasher Water Use: Facts and Figures" (December 2001), http://tinyurl.com/64u29k
2) Colorado River Authority web site, "Tips for Saving Water Inside Your Home," http://tinyurl.com/65quoc

Build a New House?
1) Oikos Green Building Source web site, "Turn to Solar for Lower Heating Costs" (December 1995), http://tinyurl.com/5plttq
2) Arizona Solar Center web site, "Passive Solar Architecture," http://tinyurl.com/5qg8jt
3) U.S. Geological Survey web site, "The Water Cycle: Surface Runoff," http://tinyurl.com/56b2vg

Use "Natural" Cleaning Products?
1) Conis, Elena, "How Safe Are Green Cleaning Products?" *LA Times* (28 April 2008)
2) Annys, Shin, "Toxin Found in Natural, Organic Items," *Washington Post* (15 March 2008)

Use a Water Filter?
1) Water Is Life web site, "Bottled Water Industry," http://tinyurl.com/56cxyf

2) Llanos, Miguel, "Plastic Bottles Pile Up as Mountains of Waste," *MSNBC* (March 2005), http://tinyurl.com/22wg94

3) Triplepundit web site, Pastor, Pablo, "The True Cost of Bottled Water," http://tinyurl.com/2gld6e

4) *McGraw-Hill Encyclopedia of Science and Technology* (1993, 5th ed., McGraw-Hill Companies, Inc.)

Wash at Lower Temperatures?

1) Carbon Concious Consumer web site, "Climate Change and the New American Dream" (2007), http://c3.newdream.org/

2) Arezki, Izri; Chosidow, Olivier, "Efficacy of Machine Laundering to Eradicate Head Lice: Recommendations to Decontaminate Washable Clothes, Linens, and Fomites," *Clinical Infectious Diseases* (Vol. 42, 2006)

3) Hogan, D.J., "Allergic Contact Dermatitis to Ethylenediamine. A Continuing Problem," *Dermatol. Clinics* (Vol. 8/1, pp.133–136, January 1990).

DISPOSAL & RECYCLING

Use Compostable "Bioplastic" Items?

1) Royte, Elizabeth, "Corn Plastic to the Rescue," *Smithsonian Magazine* (August 2006), http://tinyurl.com/65ky6y

2) Azios, Tony, "A Primer on Biodegradable Plastics," *Christian Science Monitor* (December 2007), http://tinyurl.com/6j3u67

Compost Your Kitchen Waste?

1) U.S. Environment Protection Agency web site, "Composting FAQ," http://tinyurl.com/64spy7

2) Whatcanonepersondo? web site, "Composting Factsheet," http://tinyurl.com/56nu34

Recycle Plastics?

1) Jeavans, C., "Plastic Recycling Comes Full Circle," *BBC News* (June 2008), http://tinyurl.com/57u3vr

2) U.S. Department of Energy web site, "Recycling Plastics," http://tinyurl.com/55jhdc

Recycle Metals?

1) City of Seattle web site, "Conservation Tip 17," http://tinyurl.com/66gdl9

Recycle Paper?

1) See citation 1, Recycle Metals?

2) European Topic Centre on Resource and Waste Management web site, "Introduction to Waste," http://tinyurl.com/5qgsbh

3) See citation 1, Use Recycled Paper?

4) See citation 1, Avoid Printing?

Use Cloth Diapers?

1) Holusha, John, "Diaper Debate, Cloth or Disposable?" *New York Times* (14 July 1990)

2) Sustainablity Institute web site, "The Great Disposable Diaper Debate," http://tinyurl.com/5spcgx

LIFESTYLE

Wear Organic Cotton?

1) Patagonia web site, "Fabric: Organic Cotton," Factsheet, http://tinyurl.com/56apk5

Wear Natural Fibers?

1) Patagonia web site, "Fabric: Recycled Polyester," Factsheet, http://tinyurl.com/5v6djt

Use Rechargeable Batteries?

1) Duracell web site, "Battery Care and Disposal," Factsheet, http://tinyurl.com/74hfz

2) Spencer, Jane; Ye, Juliet, "The Human Cost of Cheap Batteries," *Wall Street Journal* (January 2008)

Use a Digital Camera?

1) Bras, Bert. *et al.* "Life Cycle Assessment of Film and Digital Imaging Product System Scenarios," *Proceedings of the International Conference on Life Cycle Engineering, LCE* (2006)

Plant a Tree?

1) Jha, Alok, "How Trees Might Not Be Green in Carbon Offsetting Debate," *The Guardian* (10 April 2007)

Have a "Stay-cation" Vacation?

1) United Nations Atlas of the Oceans web site, "Air Travel Contribution to Global Warming," http://tinyurl.com/2ux628

2) Stewart, John, "Flying Shame," *Red Pepper Magazine* (March 2005), http://tinyurl.com/6rbchu

Buy Carbon Offsets?

1) Harvey, Fiona, "Warning on Quality of CO_2 Offsets," *Financial Times* (16 April 2008)

2) Ball, Jeffrey; Talley, Ian, "Scrutiny Rises Over Carbon-Offset Sales Process," *Wall Street Journal* (9 January 2008)

FURTHER READING

FOOD
Web sites
http://www.slowfood.com/
http://www.localharvest.org/
http://www.farmersmarkets.net/
http://www.bigbarn.co.uk/

Books
Michael Pollan, *The Omnivore's Dilemma*, Penguin, 2007

Carlo Petrini, *Slow Food (The Case for Taste)*, Columbia University Press, 2003

Alice Waters, *The Art of Simple Food*, Clarkson Potter, 2007

SHOPPING
Web sites
http://www.hippyshopper.com/

Consumer Reports Green Shopping Guides
http://www.greenerchoices.org/

Which U.K. Shoppers Advocates
http://www.which.co.uk/advice/greener-living/

Books
Vandana Shiva, *Water Wars: Privatization, Pollution, and Profit*, South End Press, 2002

ENERGY
Web sites
http://alt-e.blogspot.com/
http://thefraserdomain.typepad.com/energy/

Books
Bill McKibben, *Fight Global Warming Now*, Holt Paperbacks, 2007

James Howard Kunstler, *The Long Emergency*, Grove Press, 2006

TRANSPORT & TRAVEL
Web sites
http://www.greencarcongress.com/

U.S. EPA
http://www.epa.gov/greenvehicles/Index.do/

U.K. Green Car Purchasing Guide
http://www.green-car-guide.com/

Books

Pietra Rivoli, *The Travels of a T-Shirt in the Global Economy*, Wiley, 2006

Jack R. Nerad, *The Complete Idiot's Guide to Hybrid and Alternative Fuel Vehicles*, Alpha, 2007

AT WORK

Web sites

http://www.ecogeek.org/

http://www.triplepundit.com/

Books

William McDonough & Michael Braungart, *Cradle to Cradle*, North Point Press, 2002

Paul Hawken, Amory Lovins, & L. Hunter Lovins, *Natural Capitalism*, Back Bay Books, 2000

AT HOME

Web sites

http://www.inhabitat.com/

http://www.motherearthnews.com/

http://www.metaefficient.com/

Books

Alex Steffen, *Worldchanging: A User's Guide for the 21st Century*, Harry N. Abrams, Inc., 2006

DISPOSAL & RECYCLING

Web sites

U.S. EPA Office of Solid Waste

http://www.epa.gov/osw/

DEFRA Recycling and Waste

http://www.defra.gov.uk/ENVIRONMENT/WASTE

U.S. National Recycling Coalition

http://www.nrc-recycle.org/Recycle More

U.K. http://www.recycle-more.co.uk/

Books

John C. Ryan & Alan Thein Durning, *Stuff: The Secret Lives of Everyday Things*, Northwest Environment, 1997

Elizabeth Royte, *Garbage Land*, Back Bay Books, 2006

LIFESTYLE

Web sites

http://planetgreen.discovery.com/

http://www.treehugger.com/

http://grist.org/

http://www.greendrinks.org/

INDEX